Audio Mastering Secrets

The Pros Don't Want You To Know!

By John Rogers

AudioMasteringSecrets.com

Copyright 2017

All rights reserved. No part of this publication may be reproduced, distributed, or transmitted in any form or by any means, including photocopying, recording, or other electronic or mechanical methods, without the prior written permission from JR Mastering, except in the case of brief quotations embodied in critical reviews and certain other noncommercial uses permitted by copyright law. For permission requests please email John Rogers at info@JRmastering.com.

TABLE OF CONTENTS

INTRODUCTION

    Audio Mastering Secrets 1
    Table Of Contents 2
    Who This Book Is For 8
    What You Will Learn From This Book 9
    About The Author 10
    Testimonials 12

AUDIO MASTERING FAQS

    What Is Audio Mastering? 13
    How Does Audio Mastering Compare To Mixing? 14
    What's The Main Goal In Audio Mastering? 15
    Why Do Songs Need To Be Mastered? 17
    Can Anyone Become A Great Mastering Engineer? 18
    How Long Does It Take to Master A Song? 19
    Should Your Mix Sound Close To A Mastered Song? 20
    Does A Radio Ready Mastering Standard Exist? 22

AUDIO MASTERING DEFINITIONS AND CONCEPTS

    Some Of The Terms I Use In This Book 23
    What Is Headroom And Dynamic Range? 24
    Why Does A Mix Need Headroom And Dynamic Range? 26
    How To Create Proper Headroom In Your Mixes 26
    What Is A/B Comparison Listening? 27
    What Are Mid-Side Effects Processors? 28

MASTERING EQUIPMENT FAQ

    What Hardware Do You Need For Mastering?   29

    What Software Do You Need For Mastering?   29

    Which Mastering Software Plugins Do I Recommend?   30

    Analog Mastering Equipment vs. Digital Software   32

THE 8 EFFECTS PROCESSORS USED IN MASTERING

    Standard 5-Band Equalizer   34

    Mid-Side 5-Band Equalizer   35

    Multi-Band Compressor   36

    Multi-Band Spectral Enhancer (Harmonic Exciter)   36

    Multi-Band Stereo Widener   37

    Multi-Band Mastering Reverb   38

    Loudness Maximizer   38

    De-esser   40

    Volume Meter Software   40

    What Signal Path Should You Use?   42

SETTING UP YOUR LISTENING ENVIRONMENT

    Room Size   43

    Speaker Choices   44

    Speaker Placement   44

    My Personal Speaker Placement   45

    Learning And Calibrating Your Speakers   46

    Sound Proofing Your Room   47

PROTECTING YOUR HEARING

    What Is Tinnitus?   48

    How Is Tinnitus Caused?   49

    How Did I Get My Tinnitus And How Did It Sound?   49

PROTECTING YOUR HEARING

- Is There A Cure For Tinnitus? 50
- Can You Mix And Master With Tinnitus? 50
- How To Prevent Tinnitus In Everday Life 50
- How Loud Is Too Loud When Mixing And Mastering? 51
- How To Protect Your Hearing As A Sound Engineer 51
- The Rules I Follow During Mixing And Mastering 52

THE 18 LAWS OF AUDIO MASTERING

- Audio Facts Are Facts, Not Just Opinions 53
- Know The Genre Of Music You're Working On 55
- Don't Do Counter Productive Processes 55
- Always Think Natural Sound First 56
- Don't Get Stuck In Familiarity 57
- Don't Be Afraid To Make Drastic Changes 59
- Don't Underestimate Your Capabilities 60
- If You're Going To Miss, Go Slightly Over Not Under 61
- Certain Actions Have Exponential Affects 61
- When Using EQ Always Think Cut First 62
- The Lead Vocal Is Your Main Focus 64
- Listen To Your Feedback 64
- Learning Decibel Amounts By Ear 66
- Working In Decibels And Percentages, Not Fader Slides 67
- You Have To Make Everything Sound Good 70
- Let Your EARS Be The Final Judge, Not Your EYES 72
- Always Finalize On Fresh Ears 72
- Mastering Is An Art Form, Treat It Like One! 74

The 4-Band Frequency Ranges In Multi-Band Processing

    LOW (20hz-130hz)   77

    LOWER-MIDS (130hz-1.5k)   78

    UPPER-MIDS (1.5k-9k)   79

    HIGH (9k-20k)   80

    Closing Thoughts On 4-Band Frequency Ranges   81

WORKING WITH SONIC QUALITIES

    The Sonic Qualities In Audio Mastering   83

    Adjusting Your Sonic Qualities With A/B Comparison   85

    How To Handle A Song That Has Erratic Sonic Qualities   87

    What's The Difference Between EQ And Spectral Enhancement?   90

SOLUTIONS TO COMMON MASTERING PROBLEMS

    Brightness, Tone, Sparkle (UPPER-MIDS & HIGH Band)   92

    Clarity And Separation (Any BAND)   100

    Bass Volume, Boominess, Kick Punch (LOW Band or LOWER-MIDS)   104

    Warmth, Thickness, Presence (LOWER-MIDS And/Or UPPER-MIDS)   106

    De-essing (On Song's Effects Bus)   108

    Stereo Width (HIGH Band & UPPER-MIDS w/ Mid-Side EQ)   109

    Overall Volume   111

COMPRESSION MADE EASY

    Which Compressors Are Used In Audio Mastering?   115

    What Can Compressors Do In Audio Mastering?   116

    Working With A Compressor's Threshold And Ratio Settings   119

    What Are Your Compression Goals By Band?   128

    The Power Of Thinning Out A Band   132

COMPRESSION MADE EASY

Why Would You Want Less Dynamic Range? 134
Compression Mostly Affects The Loudest Parts Of A Song 134
Why Do I Never Remove Compression As A Remedy? 136

AUDIO MASTERING PROCEDURES

Should You Export Your Mix Or Mix And Master At The Same Time? 137
But What If The Mix Is Terrible, Shouldn't You Fix It? 138
The Importance of Good A/B Comparison And Mix Evaluation 139
Getting Your Songs To Translate Well on Different Mediums 140
How To Create A Cohesive CD 141

AUDIO MASTERING STEP-BY-STEP

Initial Mastering Template Setup 144
1. Let's Start The Audio Mastering Session! 146
2. What File Types Are Used In Audio Mastering? 146
3. Import Files 146
4. Visually Evaluate The Song Mix File 147
5. Use Your Ears To Evaluate The Song Mix 151
6. Slightly Compress Each Of The 4 Bands 152
7. Loudness Maximize The Song 153
8. Adjust Anything Moderately Sonically Off 153
9. Initial Master (Speaker Monitor Volume) 154
Initially Setting Up Your Bands 155
10. Setting The UPPER-MIDS (1k - 9k) 155
11. Setting The LOW Band (20hz - 150hz) 157
12. Setting The LOWER-MIDS (150hz - 1.5k) 157
13. Setting The HIGH Band (9k - 20k) 158

AUDIO MASTERING STEP-BY-STEP

    14. Check Volume And Adjust — 158

    15. Listen To The Song As A Whole And Adjust — 159

    16. Break Time! — 160

    17. 2nd Master And Tweak On Fresh Ears — 161

    18. The Final Export - Loudness Maximization — 163

MASTERING DIFFERENT GENRES

    How Do I Know The Sonic Qualities For Each Genre? — 164

    Vocals And Instrumentation May Change Your Sonic Approach — 166

    How To Master Different Genres — 168

    How To Master Metal And Hard Rock — 168

    How To Master Classic Rock — 170

    How To Master Pop-Rock, Punk, Alternative, And Country — 171

    How To Master Hip-Hop And Rap — 172

    How To Master R&B — 173

    How To Master Pop-Dance, EDM, And Synth — 174

    How To Master Movie Soundtrack, Classical, And Jazz — 175

WORKING WITH CLIENTS

    Should I Ask Clients For A Reference Song? — 176

    Using The Initial Preview As A Reference — 177

    Go With The Client's Mix Or With What You Know? — 179

    How To Handle A Very Poor Mix — 180

MY MAIN RESOURCES

    My Main Resources — 180

    Thank You! — 183

Who This Book Is For

Someone who wants to learn how to *correctly* master audio to commercial radio standards, either for themselves in their home recording studio or for their business.

You want to save a lot of money mastering your own album, or *you* want to have the necessary audio mastering skills to be able to earn $100,000 a year online!

You want all the information needed to become a great audio mastering engineer, presented in a way that's easy *to* understand.

I wrote this entire book in simple plain English (layman's terms). I eliminated all the words you never heard of and hi-tech jargon, so anyone at any level can understand and learn from this book as well.

You've invested *hundreds*, if not *thousands*, of hours into your music. If you're serious about it, now's the time to make a very small financial investment in this book so your music will sound the very best it can!

I wrote this book so you can quickly learn (in a matter of weeks) the techniques, tips, and secrets that took me over 19 years to learn!

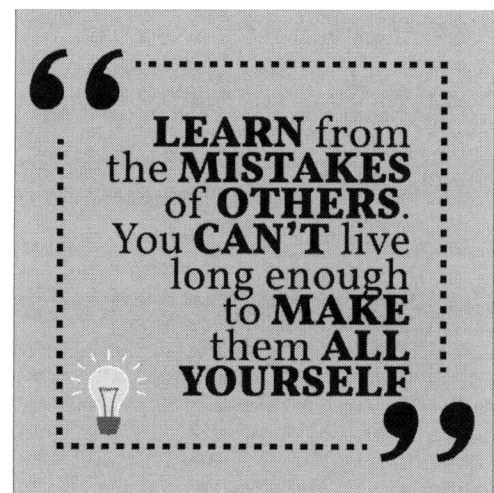

What You Will Learn From This Book

I love the saying, "If you *give* a man a fish he eats for a *day*, but if you *teach* a man how to fish he eats for a *lifetime*!"

Well, from this book you will learn how to professionally master audio for a lifetime! Then you can properly master your entire CD, your friend's CD, even open your own audio mastering business. If you're already mastering audio at your own recording studio, I'm sure you will still learn a lot from this book.

This book is a learning guide, filled with in-depth information. I wrote it from the perspective of a recording studio owner who's worked with over 7,500 satisfied clients. One reason I did this is because I wanted to cover *only* typical situations and scenarios you will experience while audio mastering, not a hundred extra pages of theory and worthless topics you'll *never* use. I included only the information you need to know.

Audio mastering is a highly technical field. There are 1,000's of different effects combinations and sonic scenarios. And when you first start out in audio mastering, you'll trial and error your way through hundreds of combinations for each song. It's very easy to get lost in technology and become over-whelmed.

In this book, I simplify the entire audio mastering process down to a handful of basic concepts and effects combinations, detailing only the ones you need to properly master music.

Also, this book was first released in very late 2017. It covers *current* mastering techniques using *up to date* gear. Since 90% of the current software plugins weren't available at that time, books written around 2007 or earlier are primarily analog gear using old school mastering techniques.

In this book, I explain:

- *What* your mastering goals are.

- *How* to use the processors involved in audio mastering.

- *When* to use them.

- *Why* you are using them.

I start out with basic terms, audio mastering laws and procedures before moving on to advanced sonic adjustment techniques and detailed step-by-step instructions. I not only use pictures, but also incorporate a few online sound and video references. **Everything you need to become a great audio mastering engineer!**

Important Note - Please read this book in its entirety. I try to repeat the most important concepts and tips, but sometimes I mention very important information *only once*. If you read only 75% of this book (or less), **you will miss out on a lot of great stuff!**

About The Author

Hello, my name is John Rogers. I'm a professional sound engineer and have been mixing and mastering at my Las Vegas studio **http://JRmastering.com**, since 1999. **I've worked with over 7,500 highly satisfied customers and mastered over 40,000 songs in every genre and style imaginable.**

Everything written in this book is based on these real-world results. Not on biased opinions, what a teacher or friend told me, what I read in another book, etc. My techniques and philosophies are backed by the great experiences of thousands of highly satisfied clients, and many repeat customers/record label projects.

I'm only telling you this because I want you to know you will be learning from someone whose mastering techniques are proven to be highly successful.

I've worked with several Grammy nominees and award winners (Bowling for Soup, Sir Charles Jones, Mary J Blige, Dionne Warwick, Ryan Saranich).

I've also mastered many billboard top 10 songs in Europe (Smiley, Nyls, Andra, Miss Mary, Mihai Ristea), movie soundtracks, videos that have appeared on MTV, and dance/EDM music that has been played in dance clubs all around the world.

After receiving *thousands* of highly favorable email comments from my clients, most not believing what I achieved with their music, I realized I have knowledge that I can pass on to anyone who wants to learn it. **This is why I wrote this book for you.**

Learn in a matter of weeks what took me over 19 long years to learn. Let's get started!

AMS 5 HR Video Course

I want everyone who purchased this book to become the very best they can at audio mastering. You *can* do it by "just reading," but if you combine reading with video examples of me mastering 10 songs live, video compression and EQ tutorials, and you can actually hear and see how I make my adjustments, **this is the ultimate way to learn audio mastering.**

Check it out at - **http://AudioMasteringSecrets.com**

Testimonials

Here are a handful of testimonials from the over 7,500 clients I've worked with since 1999. **I want you to know you'll be learning from an audio engineer that not only achieves *amazing* mastering results, but also displays a high-level of professionalism, patience, and speed.** I do everything I can to get my clients' music sounding the very best it can! And treat each project as if it were my own.

That is very kind of you to give me such detailed notes on ways I can improve future mixes and recordings.... I've been reading up on your mixing tips articles, and they are very informative, but having something that's personalized feedback on my mixes is beyond fantastic! I really want to thank you, John, again for everything, all the tips, all your time and work, you've got loyal clients here, I will certainly continue to always bring my business your way... **Aaron F.**

Every project I work on always goes to John! He has an awesome way of turning your track into something really great! I always suggest him to other producers. I will continue to use him on ALL my tracks, and I would recommend him for all of your projects! **Jake W.**

They sound great!! Thanks for finishing so quickly! **Jared Reddick, Bowling For Soup**

I don't now how you do it, but you are amazing! You are so dead on with your instincts and skills. I'm gonna drop $36 into your PayPal account. Keep the extra $30 as a tip. Go have a beer on me. An EXPENSIVE one! Wow, you have just blown me away with your work. I'm coming to you every single time, man. You are the tops. Give me a call anytime you need anything, and if I can help, I will. And when we gear up for our next CD, I'll give you a shout. Thanks again, man. You're just awesome. **Felix**

AUDIO MASTERING FAQS

Here are answers to a few of the most common audio mastering questions.

What Is Audio Mastering?

I've seen a lot of different answers on the Internet to this simple question. Some were pretty technical and confusing.

A lot of people think audio mastering is *only* making all the songs on a CD a comparable volume level. Yes, this *is* done in mastering, but it's only one of many processes, not the *only* process.

The simple answer – **Audio mastering is applying effects to a full song mix (on the stereo/main out bus), in efforts to replicate the sonic qualities of a well mastered industry standard commercial song.**

In mastering, you're adding effects to the entire song as a whole. Effects such as compression, spectral enhancement, EQ, etc.

An example of a mastering process is adding bass to a song you're listening to on your car stereo. When you add bass, the entire song gets it. You *can't* add bass to *only* the vocal track. This is comparable to a mastering EQ process because it affects the *entire* song.

How Does Audio Mastering Compare To Mixing?

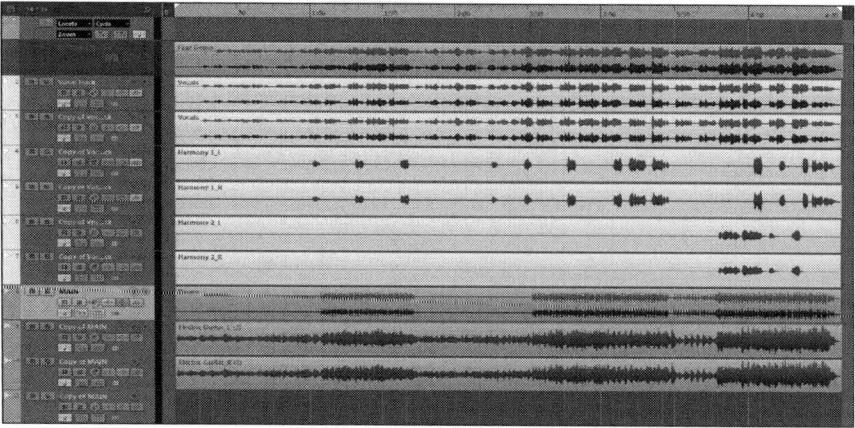

In music mixing, you're "mixing together" multiple audio tracks to create a song. Different tracks like the lead vocal, bass line, guitars, drums, etc. are being *combined* together. Then proper effects like EQ, reverb, delay are added to each track, along with panning and volume adjustments. In the final step, the mix is exported to create a song in the form of a single stereo interleaved .wav or .aiff file.

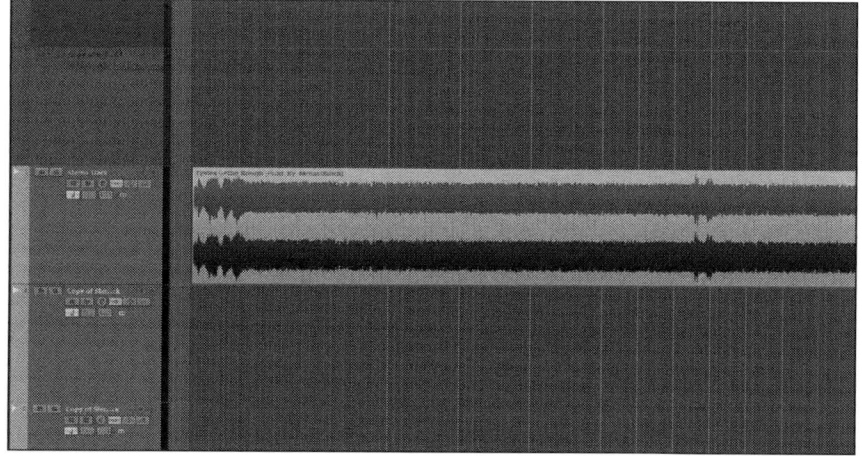

In audio mastering you're working with one stereo interleaved file. And, the *entire* song is affected by effects processes, *not* individual tracks.

At least once a week, someone uploads one song .wav file and says they want it *mixed and mastered*. **Well, you can't mix one file.** The word "mixing" is a verb and you need at least two tracks (files) to be able to mix them together. You need at least two of *anything* to be able to mix it together!

What's The Main Goal In Audio Mastering?

Your main goal in audio mastering is to replicate the sonic qualities of a well professionally mastered commercial song, in the same genre and style as the song mix you are working on.

Yes, everyone has their own slight preference adjustments like a little more bass, brightness, etc., **but overall you want to be at least 80% similar to the current industry standard.** The *only* exception is if a client specifically requests an old school master. If that's the case, then you're going to have to replicate the sonic qualities of songs from a past era.

Once every few months, a client tells me they *don't* want their songs to sound like songs on the radio, because they don't listen to the radio. That's a good reason. Ha! Then they give me a few crazy mastering requests like, "Make my song's volume level -8db below industry standard, or keep the song real muffled, etc."

My two favorite requests happened while writing this book:

Genre Hip-Hop, "I want my CD to sound soft and analog." Ok, you want me to master the first soft analog Hip Hop CD? I talk more about this at the end of this article.

Genre Heavy Metal, "Can you make my CD soft and warm?" That's like saying, "I want an ice coffee, but can you make it hot?"

When this happens, I pretty much refuse these requests. Here's why.

Every song I master is at some point going to be played along with other professionally mastered commercial songs. If the song is very poorly mastered and way off industry standard, it will be *painfully obvious* to any listener when played right after a professionally mastered commercial song.

When I first started in the mastering business, I did whatever crazy request a client gave me, they approved the masters and paid the balance. A job well done. Or was it?

The problems came weeks later after their family and friends listened to these ridiculously poor masters. That's when I got a nasty "You don't know what you're doing" email and a demand for a full refund! Even though I gave them *exactly* what they asked for. This is also why the customer *isn't* always right when it comes to audio mastering.

My Point Proven - While writing this book, a guy uploads 20 hip hop songs. I master an initial preview (like I have for 10,000 other hip hop songs) and upload it for him. He tells me, he and his producer want the songs warm and analog sounding. I tell him, no one has *ever* requested warm analog hip hop songs in my 19 year career (which should mean something). **They don't care. They know more than I do about audio mastering and that's what they want.**

So, I send him another preview with the bass up and brightness cut, a nice warm hip hop song. *Also, I noted this is wrong for hip hop.* He tells me its great, that's *exactly* what they were looking for! I proceed to master all 20 songs this way (which I mention in this book *not* to do). Ha!

The guy got and paid for all 20 warm analog hip hop masters, but I didn't hear from him for about two months. Then I get an email requesting a refund, because **he and his producer don't like the warm analog hip hop songs.** Really? I'm so surprised they didn't like songs that have the OPPOSITE sonic qualities for the genre! Shocking!!

The general public is used to, and expects, the sonic qualities of *today's* music. This is why your goal is to try and *replicate* it. If you don't, they will know it. PERIOD!

Why Do Songs Need To Be Mastered?

I've seen this question on the Internet many times. The answer I always see is "Because all songs on the radio have been professionally mastered, yours should be too." **This is a true fact, but not an answer.**

Yes, your songs need to be mastered because you want them to have the same qualities of a well professionally mastered commercial song, but this can *only* be achieved by using effects on the stereo/main out bus. Which is what mastering is (using effects on the stereo/main out bus). Many critical processes can only be done in mastering.

Here are couple of examples of why a song needs to be mastered:

- **Do you want to be able to play your song loud without it breaking up?** Then you need mastering. **In mastering**, you can compress the entire song as a whole (or in separate BANDS) so it doesn't peak too hot or distort during loud playback. Compressing a song in mastering also kind of meshes everything together. **In mixing**, you can only compress individual instruments like the bass, vocals, etc. This does nothing for loud playback nor does it mesh the song together as a whole.

- **Do you want your songs to be as loud as the songs on the radio?** Then you need mastering. **In mastering**, you can use a loudness maximizer and make your songs as loud as needed without distorting. **You can't do this in mixing** just by cranking up your levels. You will distort before reaching your desired loudness.

This question is kind of like asking, "Why does my cake need to go in the oven?" If you want it to be a real cake, and be similar to other cakes, the oven is the final process to get it there. You don't have a cake unless it goes in the oven! You only have raw mixed ingredients. The oven meshes everything together to be like other cakes.

Can Anyone Become A Great Mastering Engineer?

I would say YES, most people can become a great mastering engineer. I say this because *most* of the mixes I receive from clients are pretty good and I know the audio engineer (the band member with a computer) has only minimal training. He could easily be great if he put a little more study and practice time into it. **And if he had this book to teach him what took me over 19 years to learn! Ha!**

The bigger question is, how much time and effort are you going to put in? You know, everyone *can* be in good physical shape, or at least in decent shape. The choice is yours.

But, is there going to be a diet and exercise plan that's followed daily for months, or is everything going on eBay or craigslist a couple weeks after starting? It's up to each individual to do what's necessary to achieve their end goal.

You get out what you put in, even when it comes to audio mastering. This book gives you the knowledge and tools you need to become a great audio mastering engineer. And you'll learn a lot faster than I did. **But it's still up to you to read this book in its entirety and put in the practice time.**

How Long Does It Take to Master A Song?

I would say someone just starting out in audio mastering might take an hour to A/B compare a song and replicate it. This time includes reviewing the song on different mediums like a car stereo, headphones, small speakers, etc.

As you improve with practice, you can quickly get it down to 30 minutes per song or less. **A highly skilled audio mastering engineer can master a song in 10 minutes.** At least that's how long it takes me. Note - I *ALWAYS* split my audio mastering into *two* separate sessions so I can finalize on fresh ears. I talk about this later in the book.

Some of you might think 10 minutes to master a song is too fast. *It is* if you're just starting out. You will need more time to A/B compare and to test out different settings through trial and error. But in time, you'll learn how to quickly diagnose what a mix needs and what to do to achieve your desired results.

Now (after many years), if I spent 10 minutes or 40 minutes to master a song, my results would be *exactly* the same. An extra 30 minutes would not make my masters any better.

A good non-music example would be tying your shoes. The first week you learned as a child, it might take you a minute to tie each shoe. And you still might not get it right! *Now*, you can tie both shoes to perfection in 5 seconds!

If you spent an extra two minutes tying your shoes, could you do a better job? No. Whatever you can do in five seconds, the results will be exactly the same as if you spent two minutes.

The same goes for a highly skilled pro in audio mastering.

Should Your Mix Sound Close To A Mastered Song?

This section is basically a tip for those of you working with clients or if you plan on submitting your mixes to a mastering engineer.

DEFINITELY 100% NO!!

I've actually seen a few sound engineers online say the *opposite*. They say to make your mix sound as close as possible to a finished master. "All you want the mastering engineer to do is make the song louder." **These comments are based on common sense and theory, NOT on real world experience working with many clients.**

If the only thing your songs really needed was for the mastering engineer to make them louder, why not just make them louder yourself and save the money? Duh! No, pay someone $500 to do it in 15 minutes. I want that job!

Here's why you don't tell clients to partially master their own songs:

1. Because they're paying an experienced mastering engineer to properly do the entire job.

Here's a non-music example. Before you get your car detailed, do you clean it spotless inside and out, but leave only the windshield dirty, so that's all the car detailer has to do is wash your windshield and he's done? NO! That doesn't even make any sense.

You're paying for a car detail and you want every process that comes with it. That's their specialty and you want their expertise in every area, not just the windshield washing process. The same goes for audio mastering.

2. Mixing is not mastering. For a song to sound like a commercially mastered song on the radio you *MUST* use effects on the stereo/main out bus. When you do use effects on the stereo/main out bus you are *mastering* not *mixing*. And you're not supposed to partially master your songs if they're going to a mastering engineer. Read the paragraph above again.

3. And the #1 reason is THEY CAN'T DO IT! They don't have the knowledge, skills, replicating abilities, etc. That's why they're looking for a mastering engineer to begin with!

I explain to my clients to submit a mix that's clean, but slightly dull with lower overall volume levels. That way I can bring everything up to where it needs to be. Nothing on the stereo/main out bus.

In the past, before I was giving this info, do you know what my clients would send me? I would say half the submissions were partial masters where the clients were trying to make them sound radio ready. **The problem was they were TERRIBLE!** Way over-level, distorted, super bright and/or super bass, way too much compression, etc. Many times they had *everything* wrong!

In a perfect world, yeah send me a song that's already mastered and I don't have to do anything to it. But I know from years of experience working with *actual people* that this is a very unrealistic request. Most can't do it, that's why they're looking for a mastering engineer to begin with!

I've also heard the comment that mastering is taking all the songs on a CD and making them all sound similar. Really? That's all mastering is? So, I'm supposed to take the best mix on the CD and make all the other songs sound just like it? That doesn't even make any sense! What if the best mix on the CD sucks?

What if someone gives me only one song (which happens daily)? It can't be mastered because there isn't an entire CD?

I make every song on the CD sound as close as possible to a commercial industry standard song. Each song is mastered to sound the very best it can, regardless of past or future songs on the CD. Also, every song is mixed differently and requires different actions to achieve this. After I do this, all the songs on the CD *are* comparable in every sonic area.

Audio mastering is taking a mix and bringing it up to commercial industry standards.

Does A Radio Ready Mastering Standard Exist?

Here's another popular question I see online, always with the wrong answer! "There's no such thing as radio ready mastering!" REALLY?

Let me explain how this works. If a record label, after paying them millions, submits a new release to the radio stations and it's very poorly mastered (distorted, over-level, super bright, heavily compressed) it will be REJECTED. They will not play it on the radio. They'll tell the label the quality of the song is terrible and will request a re-master (maybe even a remix).

Technically, it would *never* even go this far because a record label executive would reject the poor master and get it corrected before the radio station even heard it.

Two Facts -

1. Some songs *aren't* ready for radio play and are *rejected* by management for poor quality reasons. This happens very often in the music industry.

2. Songs that are playing on the radio, are radio ready!

If songs are rejected for radio play, then there has to be a radio ready mastering quality standard. There it is! There's your answer!

AUDIO MASTERING DEFINITIONS

Some Of The Terms I Use In This Book

Here's a list of some of the terms and abbreviations I commonly use in this book. You're probably familiar with most of them, but just incase you're not I included some here.

Sonic Qualities - A song's brightness, boominess, bass volume, thickness, stereo width, compression amount, and overall loudness are all examples of sonic qualities.

Four Main Frequency BANDS - LOW, LOWER-MIDS, UPPER-MIDS, HIGH.

Db or Dbs - Is an abbreviation for decibels. *Decibels* are to *sound* what *inches* are to *distance.*

Q Setting - The frequency range setting (bandwidth) on an **Equalizer.** Narrow Q (16), Medium Q (4), Large Q (2).

Cut Or Cutting - I usually use this term when I talk about *decreasing/lowering EQ* volume.

Gain Down - When I use the term *gain down*, I'm saying to use the processor's GAIN function (or your DAW'S highlight and gain function) to *lower* the volume.

Gain Up - When I use the term *gain up*, I'm saying to use the processor's GAIN function (or your DAW'S highlight and gain function) to *raise* the volume.

Cut The Top Off - Some call it *brick wall limiting,* but with a high threshold. This is done with a **Multi-Band Compressor** set at a high THRESHOLD 80% using the highest compression RATIO 30:1 (infinity) or heavy 8:1 (if this achieves your goals). This technique is used so you'll be able to crank a song up loud without it breaking up or burning your ears.

Thin The BAND - A compression technique I use to remove a portion of the audio content in a BAND. A THRESHOLD of 60% and a RATIO of 8:1 will thin roughly 25% of the BAND. Changing the RATIO to 30:1 will thin 40% of the BAND.

Slight Compression - A 50% THRESHOLD with a roughly 4:1 RATIO.

What Is Headroom And Dynamic Range?

In order to produce a good master, a mix needs proper headroom and dynamic range.

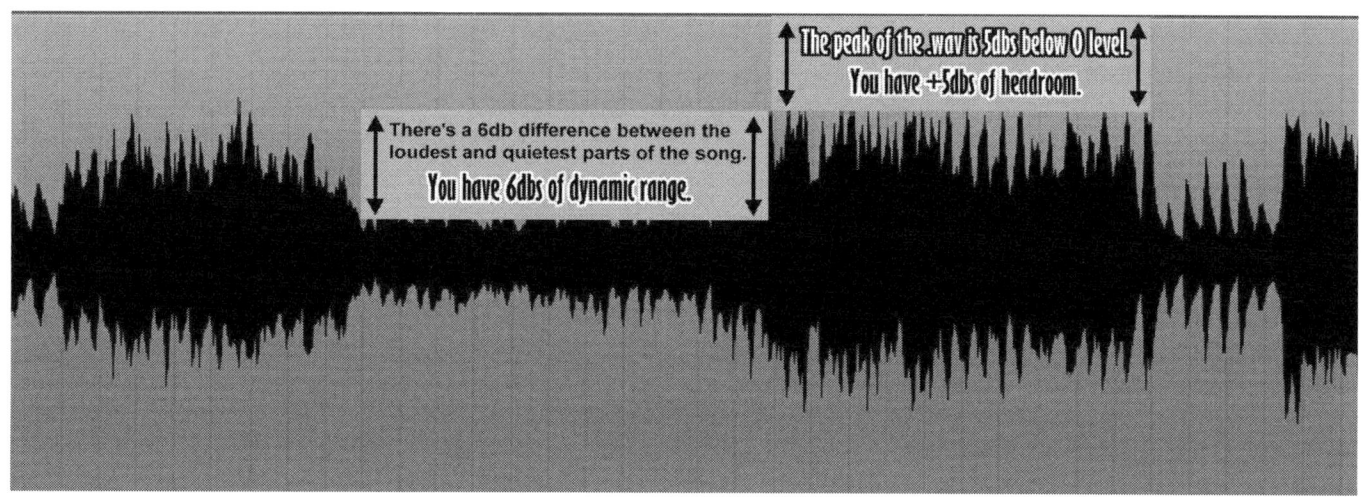

WHAT IS HEADROOM?

Headroom is the distance *between* an audio tracks peak level (when the meter is at its highest) and 0 level on the output meter.

As a song plays, the output meter on the stereo/main out bounces up and down with the music. You can see how high (loud) an audio track peaks by looking at this meter. Anything peaking over 0 level usually means distortion, **so at all costs stay below 0 level.**

How far is your peak loudness below 0 level? That's the *simple* definition of what headroom is. So, if your meter is peaking -3dbs *below* 0 level, you have +3dbs of headroom. If your meter is peaking right at 0 level, you have NO headroom.

Note - +3dbs to +6dbs of headroom is the standard recommended amount, but many times a song with more or a little less headroom can still be mastered with no problems. But, it really makes no sense to give a mastering engineer a mix with 0dbs of headroom and risk the chance that it's slightly distorted. There's no reason to do it because *overall song volume* is done in the *mastering* process, not in *mixing.*

WHAT IS DYNAMIC RANGE?

Dynamic range is the area between the peak level (when the meter is up) and the low level (when the meter is down).

Roughly, 3dbs to 6dbs of movement between the high and low meter level is a typical amount of dynamic range, but this does depend on the genre of music.

Note - One problem you want to watch out for (if you're mixing your own music) is dynamic range between song sections. You don't want a +10db or more difference between the verses and choruses. This creates a mastering problem because the verses will never be loud enough compared to the rest of the song. Roughly a 6db difference is as high as you want to go.

Why Does A Mix Need Headroom And Dynamic Range?

In one sentence, **it gives the mastering engineer more room to work with.**

If I compared a hair stylist to a mastering engineer, hair length would be headroom. If someone came in with 18" of hair, the skies the limit as to how she could style it. But, if they came in with only 1" of hair, her style options are *very* limited. **In audio mastering, no headroom limits your options.**

In the audio mastering process, a series of EQ boosts and cuts are performed. Most of the time you're going to need to boost *something*, even if it's only a little +2db boost at 100hz. **Well, if the song is already at 0 volume level or higher, you might not be able to make a necessary boost without distorting.**

Also, if a song has very *low dynamic range* (the meter barely moves) it's probably over-compressed. Which means it could lack punch, power, clarity, or could even limit EQ options. **You want your song to have some dynamic life!**

I want a song mix with some headroom and decent dynamic range. I want to EQ it as necessary, I want to compress it as necessary, I want to be able to set the overall volume as necessary, and I don't want to work with a distorted mix.

How To Create Proper Headroom In Your Mixes

To create a mix for mastering with proper headroom is pretty simple. **In mixing, never let your levels go over 0db on ANY of your individual instrument or vocal tracks.** If you do this, 99% of the time you will be under 0 level on the stereo/main out meter, which leaves you some headroom (not necessarily +3db or more but at least +1db).

Don't compress your tracks heavy and you'll usually have adequate dynamic range too.

That's usually all you need to do to achieve proper headroom, but there are always exceptions. **If most of your tracks are HOT and peaking right at 0 level, your song mix could be at 0 level with no headroom**. It won't be distorted (if not recorded distorted), but you still won't be leaving the audio mastering engineer much to work with. If this is the case, after finishing your mix, link all the channel faders together and just pull them all down a few dbs. Now you have headroom.

Remember, loudness maximization is done in mastering not mixing. DO NOT keep raising your faders way over 0 level in an attempt to match the volume level of your favorite song. This will distort it. Yes, you matched the volume level, but now you have a scratchy distorted mess!

What Is A/B Comparison Listening?

The title pretty much explains it. **You're listening back and forth between a commercial industry standard reference song and the song mix you're mastering, comparing sonic qualities between the two.** How does the song you're mastering differ from the commercial reference song?

As you master a song, your goal is for it to sound more and more like the industry standard reference song in every sonic area. You continue listening back and forth, while adding effects until you come as close as possible to replicating it. I say *as close as possible* because if the mix you're working on is very poor, you won't be able to replicate it.

A/B comparison is "trial and error testing against the reference track." That's what you're doing in effort to match it.

It's funny how this works, but after you do this a while, the industry standard reference track is in your head! You know *exactly* where each sonic quality is supposed to be and how to quickly apply the effects needed to get your master there. When you reach this point, this is when you can master songs a lot faster.

What Are Mid-Side Effects Processors?

A Mid-Side Effects Processors let you target two different parts of the stereo field. The *outside* and *inside (center)* of the stereo field.

These two ranges are preset and you don't have the option to change them, nor do you know *specifically* what the ranges are. From my experience, I would say CENTER usually covers roughly the range of L70 to R70. The SIDES are L to L71 and R71 to R.

WHY WOULD YOU NEED THIS? WHEN WOULD YOU USE THIS?

1. I use a **Mid-Side Processor** mostly to check the stereo field of a mix. I use the **Mid-Side 5-Band EQ** and *solo* the SIDES. If I don't hear much musical content on the sides (or only light reverb), the mix has a weak stereo spread and is basically a mono mix. I then either *ask for a remix* or *boost* whatever is on the SIDES (which usually doesn't achieve much).

*** VIDEO EXAMPLE ***
MID-SIDE 5-BAND EQ PROCESSOR STEREO FIELD EXAMPLE
http://audiomasteringsecrets.com/midside.html

2. Sometimes a client mixes their stereo guitars (or background vocals) *very loud* and they overtake the entire song. A **Mid-Side 5-Band EQ** can easily fix this problem by *cutting* only the SIDES down a few dbs. Or by *boosting* the CENTER.

3. If the lead vocal is buried by guitars and the guitars are stereo panned well, sometime a **Mid-Side 5-Band EQ** *boost* around 2-3k in the CENTER will bring the vocal out. You could also combine this with a SIDE *cut*.

Note - For mastering, I *only* use a **Mid-Side 5-Band "EQ,"** NOT *any* other Mid-Side Processors. And when I do use it, it's only for the few instances I mentioned above.

MASTERING EQUIPMENT FAQ

I'm going to give a few brief recommendations here. I don't want to get too much into buying hardware and software. I'd rather focus more on *how* to master music.

If you want to read more on *my* free music gear recommendations, visit -
HomeStudioGearSecrets.com

What Hardware Do You Need For Mastering?

Here's the basic hardware you need to master music:

A Computer (preferably a quad core or faster)
An Audio Interface (which contains a mic preamp and instrument cable inputs)
Studio Monitor Speakers & A Sub-Woofer
An Audio Control Unit To Control Speaker Volumes (optional but it makes life a lot easier)

If you're looking to get started real cheap, you could make a decent *hardware only* set-up for about $1,500. High-end hardware will run you roughly $3,500-$4,500. Still not too expensive.

What Software Do You Need For Mastering?

If you've mixed songs in the past, you can more than likely use that same software for mastering. As long as you can add effects to the stereo/main out bus, you're good to go.

DAW (DIGITAL AUDIO WORKSTATION) SOFTWARE

Top and popular DAW software like Pro Tools, Cubase, FL Studio, Logic, Sonar, Reaper, Ableton, etc. you can definitely master with all of these programs. I personally use Cubase.

SOFTWARE PLUGINS & MASTERING EFFECTS HARDWARE

The DAW software I mentioned above all comes with software mastering effects you could use (on the cheap). I personally don't use *any* plugins that comes free with the Cubase, but that doesn't mean they're not high quality. I don't know. On second thought, I do use the de-esser that comes with Cubase.

If you know how to master very well, you don't need thousands of dollars in mastering software and hardware to get great results. And after reading this book, you *will* know how to master very well!

Which Mastering Software Plugins Do I Recommend?

If you want to read *more* on my software plugin recommendations, I will soon have a separate website for this.

When it comes to effects plugins I love Universal Audio (UAD) plugins, and Waves too. Hardware, I like SSL and Manley products.

IZOTOPE OZONE MASTERING SOFTWARE

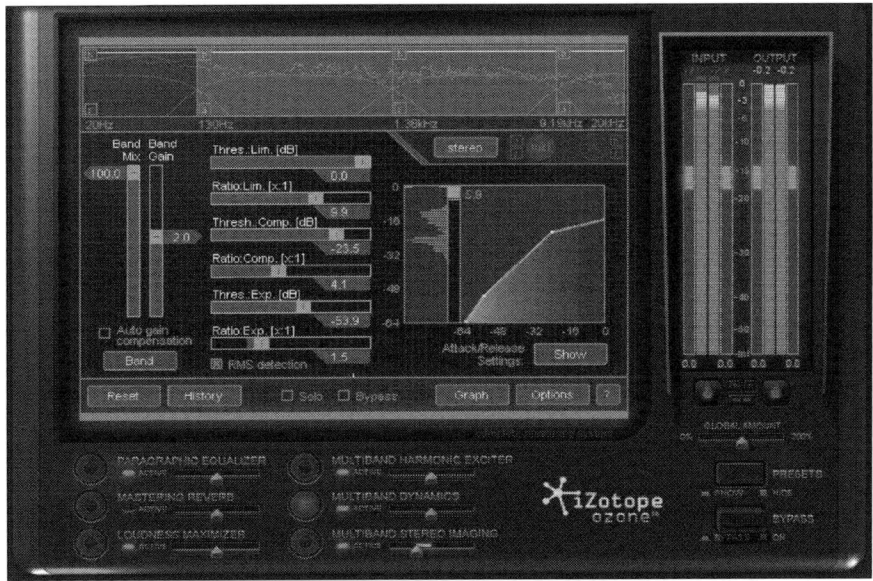

I believe iZotope Ozone is in a category by itself because of the number of hi quality effects you get at such a great price (around only $200). Not to mention the great sound quality. iZotope Ozone is a single plugin that chains together 6 of the 8 main mastering effect processors. I personally use *a couple* of the Ozone plugins during mastering, but if you used all of them I wouldn't say that's a bad thing.

SHOULD YOU BUY OZONE?

I would definitely say, "YES!" It's relatively inexpensive and even if you don't use all of its mastering processors, **it's a MUST HAVE learning tool that will help you *see* what an effect processor actually does to an audio file.** In Ozone, as the music plays you can see the audio file moving in real time. It's very easy to compress just the peaks of an audio track because you can *see them.* This also helps you learn compression ratios and thresholds through visualization.

Also, Ozone has **Mid-Side EQ**. This separates the middle portion and sides of the stereo field. What can you do with this? Its great for checking if a song mix is really in stereo, and how much.

Analog Mastering Equipment vs. Digital Software Plugins

I started my career using the old analog stuff, since that was the only option. I incorporated digital software plugins as soon as they became available, but it took many years before computers were fast enough to run them in real-time. And also before they started making very high quality plugins. Now, I use *mostly* digital software plugins, but I do have analog hardware if a client specifically requests all analog.

WHICH IS BETTER?

First off, technically EVERYTHING is digital! An mp3 and a CD is digital information that's decoded when played by a player. A rock album recorded in the 70s is *all* analog. When this album is converted to a CD, you're hearing a *digital* copy of the *analog* sound.

I guess now when someone says *analog*, they're referring to that warmer old school sound (not necessarily the gear), because you can achieve that same warmer sound using all digital software plugins that emulates quality analog gear.

I've read a lot of opinions on this. Older sound engineers in their 60's have hundreds of thousands of dollars worth of analog equipment they bought in the 70's and 80's. That being said, that's all they've ever worked with and they're not selling their gear for peanuts and switching over. Many also refuse to learn the new digital software. Their *biased* opinion is that analog is by far better than digital software plugins, though many have never really used them.

SO, WHAT'S THE UNBIASED TRUTH?

Some of the expensive analog hardware from Manley, SSL, UA does have a unique sound you can't explain. Also, analog gear can give vocals that lush soft sound that a *cheap* digital preamp can't. But now they make software replicas of *all* the old and new analog gear, and it sounds great!

IT ALL BOILS DOWN TO THE END RESULT!

Do over 7,500 clients love your work? Did they pay you hundreds of thousands of dollars? For me, the answers are "yes and yes." They think mastering primarily with software plugins sounds AMAZING! Those are over 7,500 opinions right there, backed by money!

The fact is, if you used only quality software plugins to mix and master an entire CD project, and knew how to use them very well, **the average person would NEVER be able to tell that you didn't use $100,000 worth of analog gear. Your masters would sound AMAZING and that's all that matters.**

Now, maybe an 80's old school audio engineer would notice the difference, but he's not buying your mp3s, so who cares? And the only thing he'll notice is the songs weren't mastered using all analog gear, but that doesn't mean they don't sound as good (or even better). This is like saying you know the difference between Classic Coke and Pepsi. That doesn't make one better than the other.

Also, so much of the music on the radio uses digital software effects that consumers are used to it and prefer that sound.

This all being said, save yourself some money and go primarily software plugins. The new generation *prefers* it!

8 Effects Processors Used In Mastering

This chapter covers the *main* effects processors *I* use during audio mastering. A few audio mastering engineers might use a couple more, some use less. I kept everything basic and straight forward, focusing on only the *main* settings all processors have.

If you don't know about the FREE Volume Meter Software (ReplayGain), this tip alone is worth several times the price of this book! There's a mastering engineer online selling his own version for over $100! And I don't even know if his works.

Standard 5-Band Equalizer

An equalizer (EQ) allows you to add, subtract or completely remove (hi and low pass filter) the volume level in a specified frequency range. The volume level of a song's bass, treble, brightness, etc. can all be altered using a 5-Band Equalizer.

Important Note - Throughout this book, I might refer to the **Standard 5-Band Equalizer** as "EQ, Standard EQ, or 5-Band EQ."

The **Mid-Side Equalizer** is very rarely used and is always called "Mid-Side Equalizer or Mid-Side EQ".

TYPES AND CONTROLS FOR THIS PROCESSOR:

<u>Types</u> - There are three types of EQs to choose from - **Parametric, Pass, Shelving** (I don't use this EQ in mastering).

In audio mastering, most of the time, the only type I use is **Parametric**, which is the standard setting we're all used to.

In rare instances when a song has HIGH-end hiss, I use the **Pass** setting (on the effects bus) and *low pass filter* around 20k. Then *boost* a few dbs at roughly 1 bring back some of the HIGH-end.

<u>5-Bands</u> - You have the option of turning on from 1 to 5 bands. You can then designate a frequency and Q amount for each band.

<u>Frequency</u> - 100hz, 500hz, 3k, 10k are all examples of frequencies. Most 5-Band EQs go from 20hz to 20k.

<u>Q</u> - This is the width of the EQ (your bandwidth). For example, if you set your band at 5k with a very *narrow* Q (16) any EQ boost or cut will affect *only* very close to 5k. A wider Q setting (like 3) any cut or boost affects an entire frequency *range* (4k to 6k).

<u>Gain</u> - This is used to make a frequency's volume lower or higher (boost or cut).

HOW TO USE THIS PROCESSOR:

1. *Select* a TYPE (Parametric, Pass, or Shelving).

2. *Pick* a BAND (or up to 5) and *select* your FREQUENCY.
3. *Set* your Q (your bandwidth).
4. Use GAIN to *boost* or *cut* the volume of the band's frequency.

"Mid-Side" 5-Band Equalizer

The difference between a **Standard 5-Band Equalizer** and a **"Mid-Size" 5-Band Equalizer** is how they target the stereo field.

Whatever frequency band you create, a **Standard 5-Band Equalizer** works across the width of the *entire* stereo field.

A **Mid-Side 5-Band Equalizer** can be used to target only the *middle* of the stereo field (roughly between 70L to 70R) or the *outsides* of the stereo field (L to 71L and 71R to R).

Everything else about this processor is covered in the previous section "Standard 5-Band Equalizer."

Multi-Band Compressor

An audio compressor is used for several different processes which includes compressing or limiting an audio signal.

More detailed information about compression in audio mastering is covered in the section "Compression Made Easy." This section contains everything you need to know about compression in audio mastering.

Multi-Band Spectral Enhancer (Harmonic Exciter)

All **Spectral Enhancers** have a different sound to them (depending on the manufacturer). They all achieve their sound by adding harmonics and phase correction (to some extent). This phase correction adds separation and clarity to the audio master. Some **Spectral Enhancers** do this better than others.

Harmonics allow the processor to add boominess, brightness, and warmth without adding much *volume*. For example, this means you can make your LOW-end *thicker* without making it much *louder.* An option you will need at some point.

The separation a **Spectral Enhancer** provides is quite an amazing effect. **Only if the song isn't already too bright, I always try to *Spectral Enhance* the UPPER-MIDS at least 1 unit to take advantage of the separation it offers.**

Note - The brightness, separation, and clarity this processor creates can be achieved *only* in the UPPER MIDS or HIGH Band.

If you **Spectral Enhance** the LOWER-MIDS or LOW Band, it makes it *boomier, thicker, warmer* **not** *brighter or clearer.*

Also, you can only *add* effects with this processor. You cannot *cut* (remove) them.

HOW TO USE THIS PROCESSOR:

1. *Select* your 4-Band Frequency Range (LOW, LOWER-MID, UPPER-MID, HIGH).
2. Use GAIN to *add* Spectral Enhancing as needed.

Multi-Band Stereo Widener

The stereo widening effect simply increases the perceived stereo width of a BAND. This is done by first slightly changing its phase and character. Then delay is added to the left and right channels.

HOW TO USE THIS PROCESSOR:

1. *Select* your 4-Band Frequency Range (LOW, LOWER-MID, UPPER-MID, HIGH).
2. *Select* the amount of DELAY (between the left and right channels).
3. Use GAIN to add Stereo Widening as needed.

Note - I *always* use this processor in the HIGH Band (if it's not too thick or harsh). It gives the master a little extra stereo sparkle.

I *never* use it in any other BAND. Using this processor in the bass area is of course a no-no (no one wants stereo bass). And if its over-used in the UPPER-MIDS, the middle of the mix strangely moves to the outside of the stereo spectrum. You *DO NOT* want your lead vocals and snare to be panned to the outsides of the song!

Multi-Band Mastering Reverb

The reverb effect is used to simulate space. When reverb is applied to an audio track it will sound like it was recorded live in the space size you select on the processor. Common space size options include a small room, cathedral, large hall, etc.

HOW TO USE THIS PROCESSOR:

1. *Select* your 4-Band Frequency Range (LOW, LOWER-MID, UPPER-MID, HIGH).
2. *Choose* your reverb TYPE.
3. Use WET/DRY to *add* Reverb as needed.

Note - **I rarely, *if ever*, use this processor in audio mastering.** If I do, it's a very slight amount (like 10-15% wet) in the *entire* 1k to 20k range. I adjust the HIGH Band (making it 1k to 20k), by sliding it to the left until I get to 1k.

You don't want to go much *lower* than 1k or you'll start reverbing bass content.

Also, you don't want to use a *narrow* range like 1k to 3k or it will sound tinny, flangy and fake.

Loudness Maximizer

A Loudness Maximizer is a compressor, but its main function is to make a song mix as loud as possible without distorting.

TYPES AND CONTROLS FOR THIS PROCESSOR:

All **Loudness Maximizers** have slightly different settings that use different names, but *THRESHOLD* is the main one.

<u>Threshold</u> - **This is your volume control** (the lower the threshold setting, the louder the volume of the song).

But you can't just set your threshold *anywhere* in an attempt to make your song the loudest song ever. It will distort.

Margin/Out Ceiling - This useless setting is on most **Loudness Maximizers** and has to be set at something. Most engineers (including myself) set it at -0.2db (that's two tenths of a db). Just set it and forget it.

Character (or it could be called something else on your processor) - **This setting deals with the attack of the processor** (though it is not the actual attack setting). No, this processor doesn't turn on and off since it's being used on a full song, but you could experience pumping or crackling if a song is very dynamic or you're trying to make it too loud. If this is the case, a higher (or lower depending on your unit) character setting makes the processor less aggressive and more transparent, which sometimes eliminates a pumping or crackling problem.

Mode/Shaping - This setting is similar to character. **It's a tonal shaping adjustment.** Trial and error is needed to determine what settings work best for your situation.

Dither - **Another set it and forget it setting.** I set mine at 16bit and normal, with light character, and all my masters are amazing!

HOW TO USE THIS PROCESSOR:
1. *Set* your CHARACTER, MODE/SHAPING, and MARGIN/OUT CEILING (-0.2db).
2. *Set* your THRESHOLD.

As I mentioned earlier, you can't just set your THRESHOLD anywhere.

You should have a peak level meter on the unit. You want to *set* your THRESHOLD a little *below* the top peak level of the audio material.

You can then use the **ReplayGain** software to see how loud the song master is and adjust from there.

De-esser

A de-esser is used to reduce bright sibilant sounds in vocals like "Sss, Shh, and Chh." It can also reduce any shrill instruments that reside around the 5k-7k range.

How it works is when the "Sss" or shrill sound gets too loud, the de-esser automatically reduces it. This is achieved by reducing the volume level of the frequency range where the sibilance resides, once it passes a set threshold.

HOW TO USE THIS PROCESSOR:

When I use this processor its on the song's effects bus, *not* on the stereo/main out. I use a very simple de-esser plug-in that comes with Cubase. It has an auto threshold function that works to perfection. If your de-esser has slightly different settings and you know anything about music processors, it's a no-brainer to figure them out.

1. *Set* THRESHOLD to *auto*.
2. *Set* GENDER as needed.
3. *Set* S-REDUCTION to around -7 (or as needed).

Note - I repeat, I de-ess on the song's effects bus, NOT on the stereo/main out. This way you're effecting the song by itself before other processors on the stereo/main out kick in. I guess you *could* put it on the stereo/main out, but the way I do it works for me. No reason to change.

Volume Meter Software

This software was a great invention! **It tells you the *average volume level* of a song, and its pretty much a no-brainer to use.** This allows you to check the volume level of your reference track and the song you're mastering. Then you can use the **Loudness Maximizer** to accurately match volume levels.

Also, you'll be able to make all the song volumes on a CD exactly the same. **With this software, this is one area in audio mastering you'll never get wrong!** And best of all I believe it's still free!

The software is ReplayGain. You can google it and download the stand alone version for free.

I use **EZ CD Audio Converter** which has **ReplayGain** as a function. If you're using this software - go to *Audio Converter*, import your songs, and then hit the top button *Metadata > Scan ReplayGain* to get your volume level readings.

HOW DOES THIS SOFTWARE WORK?
ReplayGain uses an algorithm to measure the overall *perceived loudness* of a song (or any audio). And it's *VERY* accurate!

A basic audio peak meter only tells you how loud the **loudest part** of a song is, which is absolutely *worthless* information if you're trying to balance overall song volumes against each other.

Most of my regular clients are pretty sharp when it comes to the sonic qualities of a song. If I'm off even 1db somewhere, many times they let me know about it.

Well, when I use this software to match and balance song volumes, they are hardly *ever* contested. A client might question the volume level of a song maybe 1 out of every 50, and even then they're probably wrong. It's that good!

Later in this book I will discuss volume settings for the ReplayGain software compared to commercial industry standard songs.

What Signal Path Should You Use?

Signal path is the order you place the effects processors on the stereo/main out bus. The audio signal goes through each processor in the order of this path.

In the setup below, the **Standard 5-Band Equalizer** is the first process used and the **Loudness Maximizer** is the final process.

I guess there could be hundreds of slight variations of your signal path, and that's ok. **This is the signal path I've used successfully on over 30,000 songs since 1999.**

On The Stereo/Main Out Bus:

1. Standard 5-Band Equalizer
2. Mid-Side Equalizer
3. Multi-Band Reverb
4. Multi-Band Compressor
5. Multi-Band Spectral Enhancer (Harmonic Exciter)
6. Multi-Band Stereo Widener
7. Loudness Maximizer (*Always* Last)

On The Song's Effects Bus:

1. De-esser (only if needed)

SETTING UP YOUR LISTENING ENVIRONMENT

Audio mastering starts with your listening environment. **If it isn't giving you a *true* sound, you'll be lost.**

Room Size

Technically, you can properly mix or master in any room size. But, I believe a *smaller* room is better than a very large one for someone who's just starting out. And when I say *smaller* I mean closer to 12'x15' than to 20'x30'. I've mixed and mastered songs for a number of years in a 20'x30' room. It took me a few days to get used to it, but after that I could do it.

The obvious problem with a big room is it's a very open space. If you don't have a good acoustic setup, the room will add reverb to every song.

You have to compensate for this on every song you mix or master, because the extra reverb you hear isn't really in the music. It's coming from the room.

In a smaller room, even with no acoustic treatment, your mixes and masters will all sound more true. They won't be discolored from bouncing around a big room.

Speaker Choices

I've used dozens of different brands of speakers in my career and I do like a few better than others. But, this article deals more with types and sizes of speakers, not with the brand choices. For *my* free brand choices – **HomeStudioGearSecrets.com**

The main mixing and mastering speakers I currently use are Dynaudio 100w powered studio monitors with 6" woofers and 1.1" tweeters. They have nice EQ adjustment options on the back and I know these speakers very well. If you get speakers that are a little larger, you'll get better LOW-end out of them, but I'm happy with the size I use.

The most important part of your speaker setup (that a lot of newbies don't know about) is having a sub-woofer on the floor between your main studio monitors. If you're using 4-6" monitor speakers, it's *impossible* to correctly mix or master any music content under 150hz without having a sub-woofer. 4-6" studio monitors will not play the low 60hz sub-bass *AT ALL*, and they're weak at best in the 100hz area.

Speaker Placement

Before I tell you the setup I like best, after *many* years of experimentation, I'd like to first tell you the setup I personally don't like (even though *a lot* of sound engineers do this). Two studio monitors, five feet apart, on a desk *two feet away from their face*. And NO sub-woofer! I think they call this "near field" monitoring.

But at some point during the audio mastering process, you *must* crank the music up very loud to set your final compression and to hear how it translates at high volume levels. You can't do this if your speakers are right next to your ears! At least I can't.

Maybe this is why the songs I get in for re-mastering badly break up when cranked up loud, and the bass is totally washed out. They were originally mastered at very low levels without a sub-woofer, and not optimized for loud playback.

I also find it hard determining the overall depth and stereo width in music when the speakers are two feet in front of me. Which makes sense. Its like watching a 50" TV. I want it to be far enough away so I can take the whole picture in. No one puts a 50" TV on a table right in front of them, yet this is done with speakers.

My Personal Speaker Placement

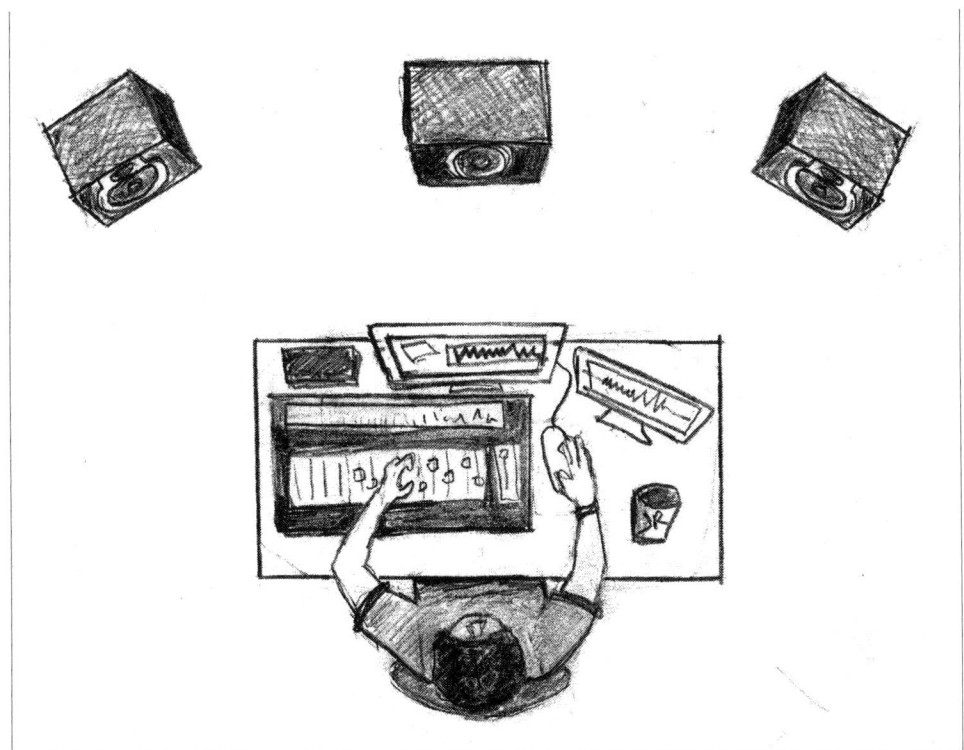

First off, I use speaker stands for my studio monitors, and the speakers stand 3.5 feet off the ground. I have the stands roughly 7 feet apart, and the speakers are about 6-7

feet away from my face. The sub-woofer is on the floor, centered between the two speaker stands.

Note - **Do not put the back of the speakers right up against a wall.** Have at least 10 inches between the back of your speakers and the wall, or the sound will be altered.

I've found this setup is close enough where I can here all the details in the music, wide enough so I get a full representation of the stereo field, and the speakers are far away enough so I can crank the music up to 105dbs to make sure it sounds right for loud playback, without blasting myself in the face.

Learning And Calibrating Your Speakers

When I first start out with NEW speakers (though I never change them now), I listen to my favorite hit songs in every genre and style. Songs that I know from my years of experience have X amount of bass, X amount of brightness, etc. **I know how these songs are "supposed" to sound.**

Most good speakers have EQ adjustment switches on them, and the sub-woofer has a volume control on it. After several listens, I'll slightly adjust the EQ on the monitor speakers and the bass amount on the sub-woofer so that my favorite reference songs sound "true" to me. I'm making my speakers sound true to life, not exaggerated in any sonic area. **Once the songs playing through these speakers sound "true" to me, then anything I mix or master will be done correctly.**

How could speakers sound *untrue* to me? An example, if I'm playing a few commercially hip hop songs and the bass sounds very weak on every song, the speakers I'm using are *untrue* because I know *in reality* the bass should be *much* higher/louder in hip hop. I know the sub-woofer needs the bass volume adjusted and maybe the studio monitors do too. And I adjust them accordingly.

If I worked with these untrue speakers, I would improperly raise the bass on every song, thinking it was too low, when in reality the speakers aren't properly playing the bass.

It's easier when working with *true* speakers because what you hear correctly represents the audio material you're working on.

Sound Proofing Your Room

I had to write a quick note on this, as I was reminded about it while thumbing through a popular mixing book that had a 15 page section on speaker resonance and room sound proofing. I must say, a very exciting 15 pages! Ha!

Way too much is made out of room sound proofing! I can audio master songs to perfection in an untreated basement, a huge studio room, in a bathroom, anywhere. I've done it all before. I can even master in my own backyard, with no walls!

Now, I would have to listen to a few reference tracks to learn a new environment. And some client feedback might be required. But after a couple hours, I could master anything in any space. At least 15,000 of the songs I've mastered were done in an untreated room. And my clients LOVED them all!

You don't *need* foam or sound proofing on your walls. The important thing is to learn your environment, whatever it is. The proof is in the number of highly satisfied clients I've serviced, over 7,500. And the THOUSAND who were totally blown away by what I did with their music.

Now, if you do want some foam or acoustic treatment in your room, buy it. You'll still have to learn how the room sounds after you install it. **My point is you don't *need* it for audio mastering.**

I've gotten in hundreds of remaster jobs that were originally mastered at studios with thousands of dollars worth of foam on their walls, and these masters were HORRENDOUS! A mash of distorted noise trainwreck! **The foam did a lot of good.** Ha!

PROTECTING YOUR HEARING

Millions of people suffer from tinnitus. A new study shows around 10% of the U.S. population suffers from it in some form, **but many have never even heard of it until they got it!** Unfortunately, I was one of those people. It can happen quickly and it lasts a lifetime...

As a sound engineer, your hearing is your most important asset. It's critical that you protect it for as long as possible. In this section, I will discuss the causes and prevention of tinnitus, and general safety practices that will help you keep your ears healthy.

What Is Tinnitus?

Tinnitus is the constant hearing of a sound when there is no sound present. Some describe it as a ringing sound, a hiss, or a high pitched tone. The sound is continual, and it varies from one tinnitus suffer to another.

How Is Tinnitus Caused?

Tinnitus is caused by either a single extremely loud sound or by loud sounds over a period of time. I know a military vet who got severe tinnitus from the sound of jets taking off in close proximity. Another guy I know got it from a single bomb explosion that was right next to him. Listening to loud music at a concert or club, if you're in a band, if you play music loud on your iPod, or monitoring music very loud as a sound engineer; over a period of time *any* of these scenarios could cause tinnitus. If you cut grass for a living and don't wear earplugs, I would imagine that could eventually cause it too.

It can also be caused by prescription drugs in the benzodiazepine family or even by over the counter drugs like ibuprofen. I heard of a man who got severe tinnitus from MSG in Chinese food. The cook made a mistake and loaded it up heavy with MSG.

How Did I Get My Tinnitus And How Did It Sound?

I got tinnitus in 1999, working on one of my very first mastering projects the day I opened my studio, JR mastering. At that time, I needed to listen to the songs much longer than I do now because of my lack of experience, and I listened to them WAY too loud.

I was reviewing my final masters at a high volume level (105-110 dbs) for about 30 minutes non-stop. When I was finished I didn't really notice anything. But, when night time came I could hear a high-pitched tone. It sounded like a 40db test tone @ 5k. I could hear the tone in both ears, but my right ear was twice as bad as my left. The first few days it was hard for me to sleep because I kept thinking about this sound. The sound was also very annoying when sitting outside in a quiet area.

Is There A Cure For Tinnitus?

No. There are many pills and snake oil products online, but I have never heard of a valid cure. But, experts say it gets better over time as long as you don't make it worse.

The first few months I suffered from tinnitus, I would say it was very annoying at night but not too bad during the day. It did not effect my sound engineering. After six months, it improved about 25%. After a year, it's roughly 50% better. Now, many years later, I would say I have maybe 20% of the original tinnitus I got in 1999 (an 80% improvement). Its pretty much gone because it was a mild case of tinnitus to begin with, and I took preventative measures so it wouldn't get worse.

Can You Mix And Master Music With Tinnitus?

Mine was not severe, so it did not hinder me at all. The noise I heard was a 40db loud test tone @ 5k. I started doing my initial mixing and mastering at around 85dbs, so the tinnitus tone was pretty much masked (drowned out). Its kind of like when someone records mic hiss. You can hear it when the music stops, but when the guitars are playing you can't hear it at all because the hiss is being masked.

Singer Phil Collins retired because of his tinnitus. Bono also has very severe tinnitus that greatly affects his everyday life. **If your tinnitus is very severe like those two, I'm sure your sound engineering skills would be *greatly* affected.**

How To Prevent Tinnitus In Everyday Life

Always use hearing protection (earplugs) when at a concert or a club playing loud music, when cutting grass, when using a blower or electric power tools, and for sure when shooting a gun. Any situation where a continuous 100db sound is present.

Also, don't listen to music over 100dbs for long periods of time. OSHA recommends no more than 1 hour @ 105dbs. **I would NEVER go more than 20 minutes straight at 105dbs, if that.** Also, be careful with ibuprofen and prescription drugs.

How Loud Is Too Loud When Mixing And Mastering?

Well, 105-110dbs for 30 minutes straight was too loud for me. I had tinnitus at the end of the 30-minute session! Everyone is different, so I don't want to give you specific sound ranges and upper limits. All I can tell you is what gave me tinnitus, and what's worked for me to improve my tinnitus 80% since 1999.

How To Protect Your Hearing As A Sound Engineer

THE GUINEA PIG EXPERIMENT

I read a study online where a scientist exposed guinea pigs to extremely loud music. The results were that the guinea pigs who listened to extremely loud music *continuously*, say for 30 minutes, had *severe* structural damage to their internal ears.

The guinea pigs who listened to the same extremely loud 30 minutes of music, *but* it was *not continuous* (roughly 2 minutes of music and then a 2 minute break), the damage to their internal ears was *FAR LESS* severe compared to the first group.

Now remember, both groups listened to music the same total time (30 minutes). But, *continuous* listening was far more damaging than *intermittent* listening.

The Rules I Follow During Music Mixing And Mastering

I initially mix and master at a lower level. I keep levels around 80-90dbs. I listen 10-15 minutes at these levels, then take a 5-minute break. I will do this for between 2-4 hours, then I take a full two-hour break.

When it comes time for the finalization (loud listening @ 105-110dbs) I NEVER go more than 2-3 minutes continuous and I pretty much split time. If I listen to loud music for 5 minutes, I take a 5 minute break before starting up again.

Above is what I've been doing since 1999 and it works for me. Maybe you can go 100dbs for 8 hours a day and never have a problem, but I'm not risking it. **105-110dbs for 30 minutes continuous ruined my ears pretty good, and I had to make sure they didn't get any worse.**

Tinnitus isn't fun. I might be going overboard a bit with my silence rests, but it's working for me. **Better safe than sorry with tinnitus because it lasts A LIFETIME!**

THE 18 LAWS OF AUDIO MASTERING

In this chapter, I will discuss what I'm calling the "Laws Of Audio Mastering." **Very simple concepts, but *very important* ones because most of them are used *every time* you master a song.**

Read through these laws now, and then again when you're finished with this book. Write them down and *learn* them all! If you want to be a great audio mastering engineer and skip a few of these laws during your mastering sessions - you won't be.

These laws will not only help you become a great audio mastering engineer, they'll show you how *not* to become a bad one. I guess you could also call this section "Mastering Mistakes To Avoid."

Note - Every month I get in a few re-master jobs. A client goes to another studio and the mastered CD they get back sounds terrible, regardless of the price they paid. Honestly, sometimes $100 a song! **Unfortunately, the sound engineer is breaking several of the laws listed in this chapter.**

Audio Facts Are Facts, Not Just Opinions

I wrote this section because it needs to be mentioned. **Audio *facts* are the same as visual *facts*.** They say, "Seeing is believing" but a lot of people think,"Hearing is a matter of opinion." Well, it's not! Yes, you can have a personal sonic quality preference, like some people like a lot of bass, but that doesn't change the *amount* of bass a song actually has. All it means is *you prefer* more bass.

1080 HDTV vs 720 STANDARD

Here's a visual example to start with. When 1080 HD TV first came out, my uncle would argue with me that 1080 HD TV was *exactly* the same as standard 720. "There's NO difference! The only difference is in the price," he used to tell me this.

Well, just because someone *believes* 1080 HD TV is the same as standard 720, doesn't mean its true. The fact is, 1080 HD has a much superior picture quality compared to 720. If someone doesn't believe this, *they're wrong!* **This isn't something you can have an opinion on, it's a fact!**

Why am I even mentioning this? Because I want you to know if you're working with clients, you will get a small percentage that are clueless and will challenge obvious sonic facts. And there's nothing you can do about it because they *think* their opinion is right.

I would say, *most* of the clients I work with are sharp. Many are very sharp. They don't know *how* to master a song themselves, but they can tell if a master is sonically wrong within a couple dbs.

But, when you are working with a sonically clueless client, their comments and suggestions are all over the map! They'll tell you their original mix is brighter than the master you boosted +3dbs in the upper-mids. They'll tell you one song on the CD is way louder than the rest when they're all the exact same volume. They'll give you a bunch of opinions that are contrary to the facts.

What do you do with a client like this? First, I tell them what the facts are. It's 50/50 whether they believe me or not. Many times I end up granting their crazy requests with a disclaimer stating I don't agree with them, and they're wrong.

Regardless of what the circumstances are, audio facts are facts. They're not just an opinion.

Know The Genre Of Music You're Working On

To be great at audio mastering, **you need to know the sonic qualities of the genre you are working on!**

Note - Later in this book I will break down the sonic qualities for each genre.

When I first started mastering professionally in 1999, I was good, but most of my experience was in EDM, pop rock, and hip hop. I knew the sonic qualities for *those* genres very well, and basically applied them to *everything* I mastered. Ha!

It worked until I started getting into heavy metal and hard rock songs, and gave them that pop / EDM / hip hop bass feel. The client's were like, "Dude, hard rock is about the guitars, man. You got the bass cranked up and I can't even hear the guitars!" Oops...

After that example, I think you get the idea here. **Know the sonic qualities of the genre you're working on!** A lot of sound engineers don't...

Don't Do Counter Productive Processes

In this section I'm referring to two or more opposite processes that negate each other. This can easily happen when you're going back and forth with different processors that can do virtually the same thing.

COUNTER PRODUCTIVE EXAMPLE

(In this example four processes are being applied)

1. Multi-Band Compressor - *Gain* +2dbs in UPPER-MIDS
2. Spectral Enhancer - *Gain* +2 units in UPPER-MIDS
3. Standard 5-Band EQ - *Cut* -2dbs in 1-6k Range
4. Multi-Band Compressor - *Set* THRESHOLD 60% (with a 5:1 ratio) on the UPPER-MIDS.

Two processes are basically EQ boosters going *up*, and two processes are EQ cutters going *down*. You're going in circles! **You needlessly added four effects that are, for the most part, cross cancelling each other out!**

This would kind of be like having a big empty glass and adding 2 cups of water, and then subtracting 2 cups of water. You're left with the same big empty glass you started with! You didn't have to do *anything* to get that result!

If you always think "natural sound first," and do a good job determining exactly what sonic qualities the song mix lacks, you won't have this problem. I talk more about this in the next law "Always Think Natural Sound First."

There are hundreds of scenarios where your effects processes could be counter productive. **As you practice and hone your craft, you will learn how to use *only* the processes you need.**

Important Note - You *can* use several different similar processes in the *same* direction. I **EQ** boost AND **Spectral Enhance** (if even slightly) on more than half the songs I work on.

Its very common to use a few different effects processors in the *same* direction.

Always Think Natural Sound First

When evaluating a mix for mastering, you should always think natural sound first in *every* sonic area. And when I say *natural sound*, I mean the raw unprocessed mix you are given. Why? There could be a few sonic areas in the mix that are already industry standard, or very close to it. Maybe the bass volume is already *perfect*, so you don't need to do anything to it. This is rare, but sometimes a mix is exactly as loud as It needs to be. If this is the case, your **Loudness Maximizer** is left at 0, untouched.

Too many times mastering engineers feel they *have to* use an effect on *every* sonic area in every song they work on.

When starting a mastering project, I always give the natural raw mix a good evaluation, noting what sonic qualities I might be able to keep. The *only* effect I use during this evaluation is slight compression on every BAND. Note - If a mix is already heavy compressed, slight compression doesn't really affect it.

If you were to automatically start adding effects without evaluating first, you might get lost in the session and start doing counter productive processes right off the bat.

Don't Get Stuck In Familiarity

Before I get started, here are some facts. **65% of the song mixes I get in for mastering are pretty good.** Using only a basic mastering template/preset (which I show you how to make in a later section) these songs will all sound much better. Not *perfect*, but much *better*.

But your goal in audio mastering isn't just to make each song sound *better.* **Your goal is to make every song you're working on sound the very best it *can*,** replicating every sonic quality of an industry standard commercially mastered song.

Now back to my main point, most of the songs you work on will not need any drastic changes. **So, you get used to doing the same things with every genre, which brings *familiarity.***

A good non-music example are doctors. They might see the same symptoms and diagnose the same disease for 20 years, and be right. Then one person comes in with a rare disease with similar symptoms, and a few new ones. The doctor overlooks all the *new* symptoms and gives the same familiar diagnosis. Well, after the person dies, the doctor realizes their old familiar diagnosis was *wrong*! They didn't dig deep enough into the symptoms to notice they were dealing with a different disease.

Technically, this is familiarity combined with laziness, but that's a whole different story! Also, my 20 year timeframe is a stretch. A very busy doctor might misdiagnose someone due to familiarity *every day!* They probably won't die, but its common for people to get the wrong diagnosis from several doctors.

A music example, for most of the hip hop I get in, the following mastering formula will work. I *add* +2 units of boominess, +2dbs of LOW bass, *cut the top off* on the UPPER-MIDS, *slightly compress* the rest of the BANDS, and *set* the overall volume. Most of the time this gives me a great master.

But 30% of the hip hop songs submitted already have way too much bass. Obviously, my masters would be terrible using this formula above, by adding more bass to them!

Mastering isn't about using all your favorite effects and presets without even thinking. I love using a spectral enhancer in the UPPER-MIDS because of the separation it brings, but I can't *blindly* use it on every song. If a song is already too bright, I'm going to either *cut* brightness or *add* bass. **NEVER** *add* more brightness with a spectral enhancer!

Someone just uploaded a project that's a great example of what mastering is. It's a compilation CD project. 12 songs, different genres, all recorded at different studios. Some of the songs are fully mastered, some half mastered, and the rest not mastered at all. Obviously, I can't just apply the same familiar preset effects combinations to every song. **Each song has different sonic deficiencies that need to brought to industry standard.**

You can't let familiarity of the job stop you from evaluating each song on a song-by-song basis.

Note - I get an email every month asking if I master using presets. FYI - If I were to use a preset template across the board on an entire album, I would never get any repeat customers. Not to mention at least 50% of the clients would request refunds. I'd be out of business in a month! So, the answer is emphatically, NO!

Don't Be Afraid To Make Drastic Changes

This audio mastering law kind of goes along with the "Stuck In Familiarity" law. **Basically, you're so used to doing *minor* mastering processes (because most mixes are pretty good) that you won't make *drastic* changes when needed.**

During an audio mastering session, most of my actions are between 0 to 3 dbs, units, k, etc. I might do a lot of actions, but roughly 80% of them are relatively small. If you master music for a living, you will experience the same thing. Unless of course you charge only $5 a song for mastering. If that's the case, ALL your changes will be drastic! Ha! (Very low paying customers many times submit terrible mixes)

So, when a song comes along that *really needs* a +10db bass boost, you won't boost it more than +4dbs because that's the highest you've gone in the last 50 songs you've mastered. **You're stuck in "minor change mode."**

Another reason drastic changes aren't made is out of fear. The audio engineer is afraid to boost or cut +4dbs or more. They're just not aggressive enough when they need to be.

Note - Once again, always fix drastic problems in the mix, if possible. The law above is only if you have no other options.

Evaluate the song mix and processes it accordingly. Do what it takes to match your reference track, even if that means making a drastic change that you're not used to.

Don't Underestimate Your Capabilities

What happens here is you evaluate a song mix, you correctly determine it's very poor in several areas, and then you don't put much effort into the master because you know the results won't be very good.

Well, I'm telling you to *always* make the best effort you can on *every* song, using everything you've learned from this book. Don't underestimate your capabilities! I say this because you don't know how many times I got in a song mix that was just plain bad, but I *surprisingly* was able to get very good mastering results.

For example, I got in a song where the bass was non-existent, the MIDS were all crowded and muddy, and the very HIGH-end was super bright. I *super boosted* the bass +12dbs, used a good amount of **Spectral Enhancer** in the UPPER-MIDS, and drastically *cut* the very HIGH-end. After all this, the mastering results were shockingly good! I achieved what I thought was impossible.

You never know what you can achieve unless you try.

I've had a lot of clients upload a bad mix and tell me, "Hey, I know you can't polish a turd." **True! But give it your very best effort!**

> *** VIDEO EXAMPLE ***
> DON'T UNDERESTIMATE YOUR CAPABILITIES
> http://audiomasteringsecrets.com/drastic.html

If You're Going To Miss, Go Slightly Over *Not* Under

Obviously, you always want to make the best audio master you can. But when you're first starting out, it's not that easy to be right on the money every time.

My point in this article is if you're going to be slightly off with your audio master, you should always go *over* for that genre of music, not *under*.

For example, if I'm working on hip hop I'd rather have a little more bass than not enough.

Rock, I'd rather have the guitars a little louder and brighter, than lower and duller.

EDM, I'd rather have the kick punch a little harder driving the rhythm, rather than slightly weak and lost in the music.

People expect to hear specific sonic qualities in certain genres and you don't want them to be weak.

This is actually one of my newer laws. **Don't fall short when it comes to a genre's main sonic qualities.**

Certain Actions Have Exponential Affects

I could also call this section "Every Effect You Use Affects Multiple Sonic Qualities."

This is something most people reading this book know quite well because it's learned in mixing.

But then again, some don't. As you practice and master more songs, you'll learn more processes that directly affect each other.

Many people think if you're working with *bass*, the song will be boomier and the bass will be louder. Those are your *only* options.

Well, in this section I explain how you can make a song brighter, more clear, or the opposite (muddy it up) using bass. Here are a few examples to give you a basic idea of what I'm talking about.

If you *boost* the LOWER-MIDS *too much*, they will run over the UPPER-MIDS and muddy up the song. So, you're *adding* bass but you're *destroying* brightness and clarity.

If you *cut* the LOWER-MIDS and LOW Band, the UPPER-MIDS will be more prominent and the song will be brighter and clearer. So, you're *cutting* bass but making the song brighter and clearer.

In both examples, you're working with *bass* and in the LOW-end, but you're affecting the song's UPPER-MIDS, brightness and clarity. **You're working in one BAND but affecting another.**

When Using EQ Always Think Cut First

If your desired sonic quality can be achieved by *cutting* EQ, go with this option. The rule of thumb is you don't want to *add* effects if you can *subtract* them and get the same sonic result. Note - This is also a mixing rule.

Now, the title of the section is "Think Cut First." **NOT*, always* cut**. I don't want you to think you have to cut in every situation. I just want you to be aware that it should be your first option if it will help you achieve your sonic goals.

The problem you will have if you don't think *cut first* is constant EQ addition. You will try to solve all of your EQ problems with EQ *boosts*.

A familiar scenario would be:

1. You evaluate the mix and *boost* the LOW-end, because it needs it. But you boosted it a little too much.
2. Now you *boost* the UPPER-MIDS to cut through the bass and went over with that too.
3. So, now the song needs a little more bass again, so you *boost* it more.
4. You're now in an endless cycle of boosts....

The result of all these boosts will be mash of noise. An over-processed (over-saturated) mess!

If your mentality is *cut* first, you'll never do more than two *boosts*. If you still have an EQ problem after that, you'll go back and start cutting. In the scenario above, you would have gone back and cut the original bass over-boost, instead of boosting everything back and forth.

The perfect non-music example is making chili. Let's say you use salt, pepper, chili powder, a little curry, and cayenne as your spices. You made it a little salty and spicy, so you add some sugar to balance it out, but you put too much sugar in. Now you're adding salt and more cayenne, etc... **If you were to keep going in circles with this, you'll have more spices than you have meat! Ha!** It will taste like a nasty over-spiced mess. Unfortunately, you can't take the spices back out in cooking (you'd have to add more meat), but you get the idea.

The Lead Vocal Is Your Main Focus

This is another law that's usually learned in mixing, but not often followed based on the mixes I get in! I think the mixing engineer *knows this*, but being able to do it (create space in the mix and put the lead vocal up front) is a different story.

With the exception of a handful of songs like "Ice Ice Baby, Sweet Child O' Mine, or maybe Can't Touch This" I rarely **EVER** hear anyone humming the *melody* of a song's music. **99% of the time they're singing the *lyrics*.**

This is why one of my main focuses in audio mastering is a clear up front vocal track, and I will do whatever I can to achieve this. I also want the vocal to have proper tone, not too bright or bassy, and not have too much of a sharp Sss sound.

Yes, there are many limitations in audio mastering. If the lead vocal is buried under five loud guitar tracks, you can't simply lower the guitars and make only the lead vocal louder. Honestly, you can't do much of anything if the vocal is totally buried. In this scenario, you might have to request a corrected remix.

My point remains, even though you're limited in audio mastering, you still need to make the lead vocal your main focus and do the best you can with what you're given.

Listen To Your Feedback

Now, this isn't a steadfast rule. There are *some* exceptions. Every once in a while a friend, family member, or client is *clueless* when it comes to the sonic qualities of music, and their feedback is worthless nonsense.

But, *most* music fans and clients you work with are pretty knowledgeable when it comes to knowing how their own genre of music should sound. They can't master it themselves to achieve that sound, but they know exactly *how* it should sound.

Sometimes they can tell you within a decibel if the bass, brightness, overall volume, etc. is off. Which makes their feedback very valuable.

When I first started mastering professionally in 1999, closely listening to feedback from my customers and friends was a big part of why I'm a great audio mastering engineer today. The sonic qualities I poorly replicated or overlooked, they would instantly notice them and point them out to me. "Hey, this song is nowhere near bright enough, or where's the bass man?"

But why couldn't I notice these mistakes? I knew music very well at the time.

Also, how do you know when a song is properly mastered? When is it done? The simple answer is when it matches your commercial reference track, then it's done.

But how do you *really* know it matches?

Below are a few answers to these questions.

1. It's strange, but when I first started out as an audio mastering engineer I knew *how* most songs were supposed to sound, and I knew *how* to A/B compare with my reference track. But, for some reason I couldn't tell if I replicated the reference track well enough. I didn't have much confidence in what I was doing either.

Again, this is where feedback comes in. With feedback, you'll eventually learn your strengths and weakness in every genre of music. You start to remember what to do, and what not to do for every genre.

Without feedback, it's just you in a room with a bunch of songs you mastered and you *think* you're great. You might be great, but you could suck and be clueless too!

Feedback gives you an idea of how good you really are, and how close you are to replicating commercial industry standard music (which is the answer to when your master is done).

2. Also, when I first started out I didn't check all the sonic qualities I was trying to replicate. Maybe once I didn't focus on overall clarity, another time I forgot to check the overall loudness (believe it or not), or I didn't compress for loud playback. I didn't always go through my sonic quality checklist (maybe because I didn't have one yet). Ha!

If you miss even one major sonic quality, you can't deliver a great master.

And remember, let feedback be your friend!

Learning Decibel Amounts By Ear

Decibel are to an audio engineer what inches are to someone in construction. Decibels are a measurement in sound.

If you want to be a great audio mastering engineer, it's important for you to learn decibel (db) amounts just by hearing them. This skill will come to you in time, as long as you pay close attention to decibel amounts as you work.

Why should you learn this? Everything is much easier if you work and can talk in dbs. Below are a couple more reasons why.

1. You can verbally (or in writing) give someone *exact* solutions to problems in a song mix. If you can express the solution verbally in dbs, you can tell a client, "Raise the lead vocal in the verses +3dbs, lower the leader guitar -2dbs @ 5k with a narrow Q, etc." These instructions give them the *EXACT* solutions to their mixing problems.

Now, if you don't know how to talk in dbs you would have to tell them, "Raise the lead vocal in the verses a decent amount and make the lead guitar less bright."

In this second example it sounds more simple, but you're not specifically telling them *anything* and they will not get it right.

And that was a *simple* example. Many times I give a client a half dozen changes or more. And if that's the case, vague instructions are 100% worthless.

Note - In the example above I'm assuming EQ is known by ear as well. EQ is another sonic measurement (specifically frequency ranges) you should learn by ear for the same reasons.

2. Another reason is your work speed will greatly increase. When you evaluate a song mix and can make db decisions in your head, it's a lot faster than going up and down with fader slides. You know roughly how many dbs the sonic qualities are off and set them where they need to be. It also reduces trial and error test time against the reference track.

I'll get a little deeper into this in the next law "Work In Decibels Not Fader Slides."

Working In Decibels And Percentages, Not Fader Slides

I worked for many years on the big studio mixing boards with 48 channel faders, before computers and DAW software came into existence. I slid the faders up and down, balancing volumes of each track against each other.

Most people reading this book will also be working with faders on a mixing board, but it will be on a computer using DAW software. You can still slide each fader up and down the same way, but in this article **I'm going to tell you why you shouldn't.**

First off, I have to answer the question, if I'm not sliding the faders how do I change their levels? The answer is, I *type in* my db amounts. I do all my changes this way. Volume, panning, effects, everything.

When using the old mixing boards, if you slid faders and turned knobs you never really look at the db amounts because they're not displayed digitally. So, you never noticed the relationship between a volume increase and how many dbs the increase actually was. All you know is the volume increase worked in the song mix or audio master.

After a while, you could listen to two different songs or tracks and be able to tell which one is louder (anyone can do this) *and* by how many decibels (most people can't do this).

But if you add and subtract decibel amounts by typing in numbers, you start to learn decibel amounts by ear. You learn mentally how loud a +1db volume increase is, how loud a -6db decrease is, etc.

Once I had a client that wanted a bunch of 0.2db changes to their masters. I'm like, "Really?" That's like asking a hair stylist, after they're finished, to cut 1/8th of an inch of hair off your entire head. Irrelevant....

And I use only whole 1's and 0.5's. For example, 1, 2, 3.5, 5, 5.5, etc. I don't use 0.3, 0.7, etc. The average music fan can't even tell a change unless its at least 1db. Many need it to be 2dbs or more. To make changes less than 0.5 is useless.

Note - I do manually move faders, thresholds, ratios, knobs, etc. around slightly when I'm tweaking the final master. But *most* of my initial work I type in the amounts.

Some processors work in percentages. A reverb processor works in wet and dry percentages. This is the same concept as learning decibel amounts. I don't just turn the wet/dry reverb knob until the track sounds right in my audio master. I type in percentages. If 10% wet isn't enough, I type in 15%, etc. Now I'm learning mentally what each effect sounds like based on percentages. Then I know where to start my reverb setting in certain situations.

Back to a cooking example. I'm a pretty good cook. I have my cooking techniques down and add spices as necessary. I'm familiar with 10-15 different spices and keep adding them until the food tastes great, and it eventually will. Adding spices and tasting is like A/B comparison in audio mastering.

The problem is, I never use a recipe and don't have a clue how much of the spices I'm putting in. I'm just shaking spice cans (like sliding faders).

Now, there's no problem with how the food tastes. It always tastes great. The problem is I could never give you a recipe, only tell you what spices I used.

This is how most audio engineers are, even some of the great ones. They slide faders and turn knobs and do amazing work, but if you asked them specifically what they did, they could only tell you the basics.

I saw a live interview with one of the top mixing engineers in the world. They kept asking him specific questions about song mixing and he kept giving them the same answer, "I listen to the mix, it tells me what it needs, and I do it. The music speaks to me." He said this several times. Ok. A true statement, but not much help. Ha! What is the music saying to you? And what actions do you take based on what it's saying?

I just saw a big time music composer in an online teaching video commercial saying the exact same thing! **"The music is talking to me and tells me what to do."** Well, the music isn't talking to us. Ha! If you can't tell us what it's saying, your class isn't going to be very helpful.

That's like asking an auto mechanic how to change your alternator and he tells you, "I troubleshoot the problem, I get back my readings, and then I fix it." Well, with that answer, you better checkout youtube.

You Have To Make Everything Sound Good

I might have touched on this in a few other parts of this book, and if I did it's still worth repeating. **These are the reasons why so many sound engineers are mediocre at best for their *entire careers!***

This is what *finally* got me to understand audio mastering and what I was doing wrong.

From 1996-1998 I mixed and mastered music off and on as a hobby. Prior to that, I composed and mixed music for several years.

In 1999, I started my own recording studio in Las Vegas. At that time my mastering was like *most* of the mastering companies you see online now. If the client's song mix was pretty good, my masters were great! Everyone loved me. But if the song mixes were below average or bad, my masters were terrible. And the client would definitely let me know it!

I couldn't understand it. I was six months in business and I could not properly master a *below average* mix. I was doing A/B comparisons, trying to replicate the top songs on the radio, but it wasn't working. What was I doing wrong?

One problem was my replication techniques were poor. I could hear how bright the guitars were in a reference song, but for some reason I wouldn't raise the levels high enough to match them. My matching skills weren't clicking.

Another problem was I didn't properly diagnose the mix to figure out what it lacked compared to the reference song. Mastering isn't just sliding faders, turning knobs, and adding dbs using all your favorite effects. But this is what I was doing.

With practice, I eventually improved on both of those problems, but that still wasn't it.

Having the constant mindset to "Make Everything Sound Good" was the final piece of the puzzle for me!

In mastering your goal is to replicate the sonic qualities of a well professionally mastered commercial song. If you *do* correctly replicate the song, it *will* sound good. **But, until I mentally focused on good sounding masters, I could never do it.** Strange...

After nine months of running my own recording studio, I changed my mental focus. After I mastered a song, I would sit back, relax, and listen not as an audio engineer but as a music lover. I love music and know how it's supposed to sound.

I would then ask myself, "Does this sound good? Does every sonic quality in the song sound great? Do the vocals sound good, clear, not too bright, like a top song on the radio? Are the guitars bright enough, clear enough? Do they have just the right UPPER-MID EQ bite to them? Do they sound like my favorite rock song does? If its hip hop, is the bass boomin' right? Is the kick punching like my favorite hip hop song?"

Or did I completely blow this master and it sounds terrible?

After of few months of using this mentality, I was locked in! That was it! **My focus was on making everything sound *good* and I didn't stop until I achieved it.**

Here's another way to explain this concept. **For me, matching the sonic qualities of a reference track was *harder* than just sitting back and judging if my master sounded like a good song.** Two different mental focuses. This is how I still master today.

Note - Of course there are some limitations. If someone gives you a terrible mix, it will never sound like a good song. It can't.

Now in 2017, my matching skills are impeccable. When I master a song, I replicate the snapshot of the industry standard song that's in my head.

During my final master and tweak, I always go back to the same mentality "Does this song sound good?" I imagine the song on the radio or at the club. And there will always be *something* (maybe very small) that can be improved and I adjust it.

Let Your EARS Be The Final Judge, Not Your EYES

The point of this article is to emphasis the fact that when it's all said and done, your ears are the judge, not your eyes.

If a .wav file doesn't have any flat spots, goes over-level and looks clean, but *sounds* distorted, it IS *distorted!!* Period! **People *listen* to music.** They don't look at .wav files for flat or over-level spots.

We can go on the flip side too. Sometimes I get in a .wav file that's completely black with no dynamic range and clearly *looks* distorted. But after listening to it, surprisingly it sounds fine. Now, the lack of dynamic range limits what I can do in audio mastering, but if I went with what I *saw*, I wouldn't have even started mastering the file since it looked over-level and distorted.

Those were just two basic examples. You will encounter many scenarios where your meters and .wav files tell you one thing, but your ears tell you something different.

Important Note - There is ONE exception to this law. **The software (ReplayGain) I use to determine the average volume of a song.** If it says 98 (which is the industry volume standard for most of the songs you will work on) then it *is* 98. **My eyes are always the final judge when using this processor, not my ears.** When I balance song volume levels on a CD using this software, I rarely have any disputes.

When in doubt, always go with your ears!

Always Finalize On Fresh Ears

Working with over 7,500 clients on over 30,000 songs since 1999 has given me a lot of experience and tremendous audio mastering skills.

I can quickly diagnose and master a song to perfection in two 5 minutes sessions. I can also master without A/B comparison of an industry standard reference track. The sonic qualities of a well professionally mastered commercial song is in my head, and I replicate it from there.

But there is one thing I cannot do!

Listen to music for several hours and then perfectly master a song. Most will call the problem burnout or ear fatigue. Whatever you call it, it *greatly* impairs my mastering skills.

After listening to music for several hours, one of two things happens to me.

1. My ears get sensitive. Bright sounds start to annoy me. So, I end up compensating and I master everything very dull. The masters aren't as bright and clear as they should be.

2. My ears get numb. The songs start sounding dull. They don't sound as bright as they really are. This time my over compensation is making the masters too bright. This is the same problem someone losing their hearing in the HIGH-end would experience.

For me it's usually #1, but that's irrelevant. I can't do final masters when my ears are in either state.

MY SOLUTION?

I always do *two* masters on each song, with an extended break in-between them. After I do the initial masters on a 12 song CD, I will not listen to any music for at least 4-6 hours before I revisit the songs and do a final second master and tweak on them. Or, I'll do the second master and tweak on completely fresh ears the next day.

Using this fresh ear approach, when I revisit the songs its like a lightbulb goes off in my head! Any tiny sonic details that I'm slightly off on become 100% clear and I quickly adjust them.

Note - I want to clarify this. I don't listen to music for at least 4-6 hours before doing the second (final) masters. But, sometimes I might master 20 songs, take a 4-6 hour break, and then do the second master on all 20 songs. I don't want you to think I'm taking a 4-6 hour break after *every* song! It would take me a week to master a 12 song CD!

Mastering Is An Art Form, Treat It Like One!

I just wanted to throw this in to reiterate this concept, because if you don't get it, you're not going to be very good at audio mastering.

I've done so many re-mastering jobs since 2010. If you look up "online mastering" or "cd mastering" on Google, **I've gotten re-mastering jobs from at least 8 of the top 10 studios listed,** a few several times. What they gave their clients was an absolute joke! And an automated mastering site like LANDR, I get a few of those to re-master every week. I know this because they automatically put LANDR in their file names.

Why is this happening? They're just flipping switches, using cheap automation software or presets, working on burned out ears, just in it for the money, and they're obviously not focusing on making every song sound good.

They're breaking half of my audio mastering laws!

CHECK OUT THIS .WAV FILE!

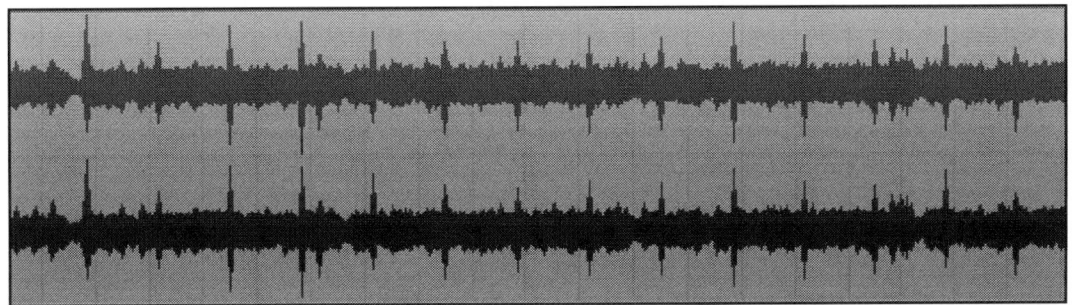

Here's a story for you. A client sends me this rock song for mastering and tells me it was recorded at one of the biggest recording studios in all of Canada. This studio worked with some of the biggest names in rock in the 80's.

Notice anything strange by just looking at it? First off, the left and right channels are 100% identical! This song is MONO. Also, why does a rock song have these little peaks? Those are thin snare drum hits.

Listening to this song, the mids are over-compressed and hissy, the snare is thin, and the song is in MONO. You can't have a MONO rock song! Obviously, I rejected this song for mastering. Even if the song was properly compressed, wasn't hissy and the snare was thick, the studio still gets an "F" for delivering a MONO rock song! **Many mastering laws were broken here.**

If you want to be good at this, you have to look at it as an art form. Unless you're one of those artists that just randomly throws paint on a canvas and is done in 5 minutes, great artists take all the time they need to create a great work of art. And, they take great pride in their work. The Mona Lisa took roughly 14 years to paint!

Now, I'm not saying to take a week to master one song. **My point is to take the time you need to deliver great work. Don't just flip faders, use presets, rush your projects, and deliver crap.**

Treat people how you want to be treated, and strive for excellence in all you do. Why not? **FYI - You'll never get a repeat customer if you don't!**

The 4-Band Frequency Ranges In Multi-Band Processing

In this book, many times I've mentioned that audio mastering is an *overall* process. It affects a song *as a whole*. If you make a song louder, the *entire* song is made louder, you can't make *only* the lead vocal track louder. This is true.

But the concept "affects a song as a whole" technically isn't entirely true. I explained it that way to start because I didn't want any confusion between mixing and mastering.

The truth is, the 4-BAND frequency ranges used in audio mastering splits a song into four independent parts. This gives you a little more flexibility when making adjustments.

THE 4-BAND FREQUENCY RANGES IN MULTI-BAND PROCESSING

Several of the processors used in audio mastering are multi-band processors, which work within the four frequency bands (LOW, LOWER-MID, UPPER-MID and HIGH). You have control over the frequency range each BAND covers, but there are basic settings for these BANDS that most people use (at least initially). I will go over the initial frequency range setting for each BAND in the upcoming pages.

These BANDS are the reason why audio mastering technically is not an overall process, since you can work independently with them. For example, with a **multi-band compressor** you can *slightly* compress *only* the LOW Band, but compress the UPPER-MIDS *very heavy*.

Using a **"*single-band*" compressor**, if you add heavy compression, the *entire song* is compressed heavy, *not* just a specific frequency BAND.

As you can see, multi-band processors give you more options and flexibility. Its like comparing a regular one-speed bike to a 10-speed bike. Even if you don't use all 10 gears, you still have them if you need them. The one speed bike, you're limited to one option.

Important Note - On the upcoming pages, I give you several tips but unless you SOLO each BAND it will be difficult to analyze them. During your A/B comparisons, be *sure* to SOLO each BAND on the song you're mastering *and* your reference track.

LOW (20hz-130hz)

This frequency range is the absolute BOTTOM-end of the song. This BAND is where you'll find punch, bass boominess, and hip hop sub-bass. Also, the lower range of the bass guitar/synth resides here too.

How This BAND Should Sound -

You want to make sure your *boominess* and bass *loudness* are correct for your genre. That's pretty much the whole ballgame in this BAND.

Unless you make the bass way too loud, this BAND is too far away from the UPPER-MIDS to run them over and muddy up the song.

I almost *never* need to compress this BAND other than my standard slight amount.

Common Problems In This Area -

Many times the mixer does not properly high-pass filter the bass guitar/synth and leaves too much of it in this range. If that's the case, it might run over the kick and phase it out. A phased out kick will lose its punch and the entire BAND will sound like a big muffle.

Surprisingly, sometimes an improperly filtered bass guitar/synth cancels out the kick so much you can barely hear it, even though its volume was not lowered during mixing. This *cannot* be corrected in mastering and must be fixed in the mix.

LOWER-MIDS (130hz-1.5k)

This frequency range is just below the middle of the song. It's where you'll find a song's bass line, thickness and warmth (the body of a song).

How This BAND Should Sound -

This BAND should be clear (not muffled), but warm and thick enough so it complements the rest of the song.

The LOWER-MIDS work with the bright UPPER-MIDS to balance out the song. If they're weak or thin, the UPPER-MIDS take over and the song is tinny and too bright. If they're too strong, they could run over the UPPER-MIDS creating a muddy master. You want to get this BAND just right.

This BAND usually gets only slight compression, unless it's problematic (muffled, thick, harsh).

Possible Problems In This Area -

A few instruments and the lower range of the vocal tracks all reside in this area. If these tracks are not properly high and low pass filtered during mixing, this can create a huge muffle, an element of harshness, or even vibration that's so loud it overtakes the entire song.

I've had great success eliminating this problem by thinning out the BAND. I talk about this in detail later in the book.

On the flip-side, sometimes this BAND is very thin. If that's the case, I *thicken* it up with the **Spectral Enhancer** and possibly *boost* up its volume using the **Multi-Band Compressor**.

UPPER-MIDS (1.5k-9k)

This frequency range is just above the middle of the song.

This is where a song's brightness and overall clarity comes from. Roughly 75% of the vocals, guitars, and music melody resides here (the main focus of a song).

How This BAND Should Sound -

With all this content, this BAND is the most important in audio mastering. When I start a mastering project, my first step is to make this BAND sound right. The other three BANDs compliment it to make a great audio master. Kind of like in mixing, most people start with the kick/bass. In audio mastering, I start with the UPPER-MIDS.

I want this BAND to have proper brightness and clarity compared to an industry standard song.

Also, this BAND is where proper compression is crucial to prevent the song from breaking up, or burning your ears on loud playback.

Possible Problems In This Area -

Out of the 4-BANDS, this one is *by far* the most problematic. So many different tracks reside here. This makes it difficult during mixing to create space, which many times leaves a mash of noise. Just solid heavy saturated bright UPPER-MID noise.

But, the biggest problem I see in this range is the vocal being completely smashed or run over by the music in sections of the song. Or the vocal track is mixed too low (a trick poor singers use). But this trick doesn't work if you can't understand 75% of what's being sung!

Also, this BAND is the listener's primary focus. So, any problems are easily noticed and magnified.

Later in this book, I explain options to correct these problems. I also cover proper compression in this BAND as well.

HIGH (9k-20k)

This frequency range is the very highest range of the song. This is where you'll find the top-end of the hi hats, cymbals, chimes, etc.

Though it doesn't have much music content, it still makes a difference in the song. Many times I use the HIGH Band to add that extra sparkle that's missing.

How This BAND Should Sound -

Similar to the LOW Band, the HIGH Band is mostly about *volume*. You want to get the volume right compared to the rest of the song.

Also, you want to make sure you can hear the hi hats well, since they drive the rhythm of the song.

This BAND *always* gets only slight compression.

I also *always* slightly **Stereo Widen** this BAND (unless its problematic). I talk more about this at a later time.

Possible Problems In This Area -

If the hi hats or cymbals are mixed way too loud or thick, you'll have a problem here. Gaining this area *down* using the **Multi-Band Compressor** is the easy solution. An **EQ cut** can also do the trick.

Closing Thoughts On 4-Band Frequency Ranges

Here's an important note I must mention. **Your *initial* frequency range settings (like LOW 20hz-130hz) are *not* set in stone.** Sometimes you might need to slide a range over a bit to include more of the adjacent BAND'S frequency range. **Be sure to SOLO the BAND while sliding it over.**

One example would be if you had a deep male vocal and wanted to compress it more, without affecting the *entire* LOWER-MID Band. In this scenario, you would *slide* the UPPER-MID range to the *left* (from 1.5k to 1k) to include a little more of the deep male vocal that resides there. This would mean the LOWER-MIDS now have a new end point at 1k, *not* 1.5k. I also do this to include a little more LOWER-MID frequency instrumentation if needed.

Another common slide is LOW Band *right,* maybe up to 250hz. The goal here is to include more of the bass guitar/synth so I can Spectral Enhance it to *add* some boominess, or volume *boost* the BAND to make the bass guitar/synth louder.

Note - **Obviously, these common examples are *only* if you need to achieve these sonic qualities.** I'm not saying to *always* do this! My main point is, **remember you have the option to move any range over left or right as needed.**

Important Note - I repeat, be sure to SOLO the band while you are sliding it over. You have to clearly be able to hear what is being included in the new BAND you are creating.

Also, sometimes using your realtime meters allows you to see how much to slide your BAND range over. You might be able to see the rhythm or vocal you're looking for jumping up and down in the adjacent BAND.

How often do *I* need to slide these initial ranges around and change them? I would say maybe 50% of the time I slightly change one of the BANDS. The other 50%, I use all of the BAND ranges as given in this book.

How far do I move these ranges? Usually 1k. 2k is a big slide. The only time I go 3k is in the HIGH Band when I *slide* it to 7k to reduce harsh high hats and cymbals.

You'll see later in this book that my entire thought process in audio mastering works with these 4-BANDS. I work with each BAND one-by-one (starting with the UPPER-MIDS) and get them to an industry standard level. **If each BAND is right, the whole song will be too!**

WORKING WITH SONIC QUALITIES

In this section I will cover the sonic qualities you're trying to replicate in audio mastering. It includes a basic overview of the sonic qualities you will be working with, how to adjust them, how to handle a song with erratic sonic qualities, and the differences between 5 Band EQ and Spectral Enhancement.

The Sonic Qualities In Audio Mastering

When you master a song, your goal is to match a well mastered commercial song. **During a mastering session you need to A/B compare each sonic quality one at a time.**

After 18+ years, I still mentally run through my entire sonic quality checklist. This is a must!

For example, does the song have too much or not enough boominess, brightness, bass volume, etc.? If I don't do this, eventually I'll start missing sonic qualities to the point where my masters start sounding poor, and I'm no longer a great mastering engineer.

This section is an overview of the sonic qualities in audio mastering. **When you breakdown your reference track for A/B comparison, these are the sonic qualities you are trying to match.** I included a few notes for each one. Later in this section, I explain everything in greater detail.

Clarity & Separation (Any BAND)

Clarity and separation differs from brightness and tone, though many don't understand this. I have a great non-music example that explains this.

Let's say your vision is poor and you wear glasses. You're watching TV with your glasses *off* and the picture is blurry. You can go up to the TV and make the picture brighter and use contrast to adjust the tone, but it will still look blurry to you, with objects blending together. Maybe a little clearer, but nothing drastic.

Once you put your glasses on, now you have clarity and separation between the objects on the screen. Brightness and contrast only brought a slight bit of clarity improvement. The glasses were the solution.

Brightness & Tone, Sparkle (UPPER-MIDS & HIGH Band)

This is the first step I take in the mastering process. I want to initially get my brightness, tone, and sparkle somewhat close to industry standard, so I can work everything else around it.

This sonic quality also includes the opposites (dull, lifeless, flat, tinny).

Bass Volume, Boominess, Kick Punch (LOW Band or LOWER-MIDS)

Remember, I'm not saying to necessarily *add* boominess, some genres like hard rock don't have much. I'm saying to check the bass volume, boominess, and kick punch so they're correct, matching your commercial reference song.

Warmth, Thickness, Presence (LOWER-MIDS or UPPER-MIDS)

ALL songs need *some* thickness and presence. No genres are thin and tinny unless it's a ukulele solo. How much warmth you need depends on the genre. With classic rock your focus is on warmth. But with heavy metal or hip hop, not at all.

Unless of course you have the client, like I did, who wanted soft warm hip hop masters. Ha! But then again, he wanted a refund too after I did what he asked for. (I told this story very early in the book)

This sonic quality also includes the opposites (harshness, thinness, distortion, etc).

Compression, Dynamics (UPPER-MIDS, LOWER-MIDS, or Overall)

You want proper compression and as much dynamic range as possible (after meeting your genre's overall volume level). **See the upcoming section "Compression Made Easy."**

De-essing (On song's effects bus)

If the Ssss sound is too bright on the vocal tracks, usually you can de-ess the entire song a bit in the mastering process and not affect the instruments. But if it does affect them (dull them too much), request a remix with the vocals de-essed.

Stereo Width (HIGH Band and/or UPPER-MIDS)

I always **Stereo Widen** the HIGH Band a bit, and use **Mid-Side EQ** (Side Only) in the UPPER-MIDS if I need to *boost* the stereo field. You can also add in a **Single Band Stereo Widener** (on the song's track bus) as another option.

Overall Volume (Overall)

Use **ReplayGain** to check your song's overall loudness, and then use your **Loudness Maximizer** to get it where it needs to be.

Adjusting Your Sonic Qualities With A/B Comparison

In my first year of professional mastering, I frequently used the A/B comparison technique. Which is basically trial and error with your mastering settings, in effort to match a commercial reference track. As I got better, my initial mastering actions were are lot closer to where they were supposed to be (much less error).

Now, I still audition and tweak different sonic qualities, but my decision making is almost instantaneous, as opposed to when I first started out (when I might spend 20 minutes trying to decide if the bass was right or not).

Now I can listen to three different bass settings and decide in literally under 5 seconds which one is best for the song.

THE A/B COMPARISON PROCESS

When trying to replicate the sonic qualities of a reference track, I determine what the song mix I'm working on lacks and I try to match it. We all know this. **But when I apply the remedy, I always go high and then low, trying to determine what sounds best.** It's basically moving around your settings, using trial and error to decide what works best.

For example, if I *know* the song I'm mastering needs more bass loudness, I'll try a big +5db boost and listen, then a +3db boost, and then +1db. Which one sounds best? Which one matches my reference track? **Also, does it work well with the song as a whole?**

*** VIDEO EXAMPLE ***
ADJUSTING YOUR SONIC QUALITIES WITH A/B COMPARISON
http://audiomasteringsecrets.com/compare.html

I also had to mention this. **Don't match the bass (or any sonic quality) of your reference track if it runs over your entire song!** All sonic qualities have to work together. You have to take into consideration the song you're working on as a whole.

Also, this is common sense but I had to give it a quick mention. I don't want anyone to think they can just take the preset settings and remedies I give in this book, blindly apply them "as is," and their songs are mastered to perfection.

Important Note - When matching sonic qualities to a commercial industry standard reference track, you match them one by one, but remember you're mastering the entire song as a whole. **And it has to sound good as a whole.**

For example, if your song has no bass (and you can't correct it), you can't try and match only the brightness quality of the reference track. The reference track's brightness has its bass amount factored in when it was mastered. Yours doesn't have any bass.

This is like making chocolate milk but you don't have all the ingredients. The chocolate milk recipe calls for 2 cups of milk and 6 tablespoons of chocolate syrup. If you have only a 1/2 cup of milk, you can't match the 6 tablespoons of chocolate syrup and think it's going to work. Unless you really like chocolate!

How To Handle A Song That Has Erratic Sonic Qualities

This answer was tough for me to put into words, but it's probably one of the most important in this book.

First off, exactly what am I talking about? Sometimes the sonic qualities of a song mix change drastically from section to section. There's no consistency in them. What do you do when this happens?

MAKING COMPENSATING DECISIONS BETWEEN SONG SECTIONS

Like I always say, a song mix isn't *one* mix, it's *several* mixes. Most novice sound engineers treat it as one, but it's not.

All songs have sections. Songs have an opening, verses, sometimes pre-choruses, choruses, a bridge, and then the big finale ending. Each section needs to be mixed separately with different effects, different track volumes, etc. You can't just keep adding more and more instruments using the same effects and volume levels. You'll be left with a huge mash of noise by the time you get to the big finale ending! But most engineers do this, and it creates a big problem. Note - This is a mixing issue for another day, but needed to be mentioned to setup the rest of this article.

SO, HOW DOES THIS PERTAIN TO AUDIO MASTERING?

The problem is when the sonic qualities in each section are all over the map. For example, the VERSES & PRE-CHORUSES are very dull and thin, the CHORUSES are medium bright, and the FINALE is a super bright thick mash of noise!

In audio mastering, I can't make 1/3 of a song brighter, 1/4 of a song duller, and then leave the rest of the song "as is." If I *boost* UPPER-MID **EQ** or **Spectral Enhance** it, EVERY SECTION gets it! The dull sections are now bright, *and* the super bright sections are now impossible to listen to.

If you run into this problem, you can't make a *great* master. You can make the raw mix sound *better*, but *great* is tough because you have to compensate between sections and do the best you can.

WHEN I'M FACED WITH THIS PROBLEM, I FOLLOW THESE RULES:

First off, with **EVERY** audio mastering project, I move the playback cursor around and evaluate the sonic qualities of each section. I give a quick listen to the loudest part of the song, the verses, choruses, etc. Obviously, if I don't closely review each section, I would never even know if they were erratic!

1. When making these compensations, I don't want any part of the song to sound terrible, grade "F." Let's say a song has three sections with very distinct sonic qualities. **I'm going to try and master the song so it sounds the best it can *overall*.**

Using a grading scale, each section cannot be mastered "A-A-A" because they're too drastically different. But, I would rather the song sections be mastered to a quality grade level of "C-C-C" than "A-C-F." Yes, the "A" part of the song would sound amazing, but when the "F" section comes on, that's when the client requests a refund. Ha!

Now, I'm not saying that "C-C-C" is even achievable. **My point is, average overall beats terrible for a short time!**

Another option is to master the song "A-C-F," and then tell the client what they need to do to fix the "F" parts. But like I mentioned earlier in this book, more times than not, they can't do it. They'll send you back a re-mix that's almost exactly the same.

2. Another rule is to put most of your efforts into the *longest* parts of the song. For example, if 70% of a song is dull and 30% is bright, I'm going to make the song brighter and cater to the 70% of the song. In this scenario, I will try to get 70% grade "A" and 30% "C-." I never master any parts to grade "D" or lower. "C-" is the lowest I will go.

Important Note - I hate to add any confusion, **but most of the time (but not always) the brightest parts in a song mix are *also* the loudest parts**, which is a good thing.

Sometimes you can compress them heavy to remove the brightness (in the loudest parts), and then make the song brighter overall (which then corrects the lower volume dull parts). This is actually a common occurrence and remedy I use often, since so many people have super loud bright choruses.

3. Here's an advanced solution I rarely use, but it is another option. In audio mastering you add effects to the stereo/main out. Well, you could take the song .wav file and cut it up section by section, and then put the sections on different tracks.

Now that you have each section on a different track, you can apply effects (like EQ) to the *song's track bus* and work with each specific individual section. This is a lot of work, but it is an option if you desperately need it.

An easy way to do this is to make cuts in the song's .wav file before and after each section you want to work with, copy this track as many times as necessary, and then delete what's not needed. For example, my first track I delete everything *but* the VERSES (leaving only the verses), the next I delete everything *but* the CHORUSES, and so on.

What's The Difference Between 5-Band EQ And Multi-Band Spectral Enhancement?

Since **EQ** and **Spectral Enhancement** have similar processing qualities, and both can be used to make a song brighter and sometimes clearer, I'm going to explain the main differences between the two.

I would say I use **5-Band Standard EQ** in 100% of the songs I master. Even if it's 1db somewhere, it's used. **Spectral Enhancement**, I use probably 80% of the time. If I don't use it in the UPPER-MIDS, because they're already too bright, I might still use it in the LOW-end to counteract the brightness.

Lastly, if my UPPER-MIDS aren't already too bright, it's very common for me to use **both processors** on them. **Spectral Enhancement** for clarity, separation, and brightness and **5-Band Standard EQ** to add more brightness, but mainly to shape the tone of the brightness.

Will I ever cut HIGH-end EQ and then Spectral Enhance that same area? Which are technically opposite processes. Great question! The answer is, yes (though not very often). If I have a super bright mash of noise in the UPPER-MIDS, I might *cut* it with **EQ**, and then **Spectral Enhance** it a bit to try and benefit from the processors clarity & separation properties. Does it work? Sometimes, but I won't know unless I try.

Spectral Enhancement	Equalization
1. A Spectral Enhancer can only *add* effects, not *cut or reduce* them.	**1.** You can *add* OR *cut* frequency volumes using EQ.
2. You can add phase correction which "magically" creates track separation and clarity in a mix. Note - *Only* in the UPPER-MIDS and HIGH Band. Adding it to the LOW-end creates boominess.	**2.** If you make a song brighter with EQ, technically clarity could be improved, but true track separation *does not* come with it.
3. Using harmonics, you can *add* boominess, thickness, or warmth to your bass without adding much volume to it. Also, harmonics can *create* bass from a weak source.	**3.** You can *boost* the bass volume of what's there (and sometimes that's all you need). But since EQ doesn't add harmonics you're not actually *creating* anything.
4. Works *only* within the 4-Band Frequency Ranges (LOW, LOWER-MID, UPPER-MID, HIGH). Anything you do affects the entire BAND.	**4.** You can select up to 5 band positions at any frequency and create any range you like (using Q). This is why even if I use the Spectral Enhancer, I *always* use EQ too for detailed frequency tonal shaping.
5. Can brighten up the UPPER-MIDS and HIGH Band. But it must be the entire BAND.	**5.** Can also brighten up the UPPER-MIDS and HIGH Band area, but not limited to those BANDS as a whole. For example, you could just *boost* 5k +6dbs.

A Multi-Band Compressor can also be considered an EQ because it can create a volume change in a frequency range when using GAIN or THRESHOLD/RATIO. But that's a different topic I cover in "Compression Made Easy" and "Audio Mastering Step-By-Step."

SOLUTIONS TO COMMON MASTERING PROBLEMS

In this section I will cover common sonic quality problems you will encounter in audio mastering and how to fix them. Problems like a song being too bright, harsh, tinny, not boomy enough, not loud enough, etc.

Brightness, Tone, Sparkle (UPPER-MIDS & HIGH Band)

Brightness, tone, and sparkle are some of the most important sonic qualities in the audio mastering process. The vocals, lead guitar, synths, and music melody are often the main focal points of a song, which makes getting these elements correct very critical.

We all know what brightness and sparkle is. But the "tone" of the brightness is something a little different. I guess a similar comparison of tone would be the contrast control on a TV.

A good music example is the lead guitar in a rock song. When mastering a rock song, I have to use the right combination of **Spectral Enhancement** and **Standard 5-Band EQ** in the UPPER-MIDS, so the guitars have a nice tone (bite) to them. An **EQ** *boost* between 3k to 6k changes a guitar's tone. Sometimes I might *boost* only 4k with a narrow Q to achieve the proper tone I'm looking for, or even the entire 4k to 6k range.

Most of the time I employ a staggered range. Example, *boost* +2db at 3k (narrow Q), and then +6db at 6k (medium Q). Whatever gives me the bright tonal bite I'm looking for. Its trial and error with the **Standard 5-Band EQ** and the **Spectral Enhancer** until I find it.

DIAGNOSIS AND REMEDY

Some or *all* of the actions given might need to be taken to solve your sonic problem. Decide which processes to use, trial and error with them, and then a little tweaking of the settings will be necessary. **What I'm trying to say is, these aren't blind "set it and forget it" presets.**

PROBLEM - NOT BRIGHT ENOUGH

You're going to either add brightness or remove mud (anything that conflicts with brightness). Sometimes you need to do both actions.

Important Note - Before applying any of these actions, when you first start out, make sure your **Multi-Band Compressor's** THRESHOLD and RATIO settings aren't cutting brightness in the UPPER-MIDS. You don't want to do counter productive processing. Remember, natural sound first.

Processor	Control	Action	Location	Notes
Spectral Enhancer	Gain	Boost	UPPER-MIDS	I always try to *add* at least one unit of spectral enhancing (if possible) to every song for the clarity and separation it brings. *Add* more if needed for brightness.
Standard 5-Band Equalizer	Gain	Boost	3k to 6k	Move around this range or use the entire range to achieve your desired brightness and proper tone. *Boost* as needed. Note - Many times I employ a staggered range. Example, *boost* +2db at 3k and +5db at 6k. This might give me the nice bright tone I'm looking for.

Standard 5-Band Equalizer	Gain	Boost	4k-10k Range	This is rare, but every once in a while I'll get a song that's total mud, with a very weak HIGH-end. After *cutting* the bass a bit, I administer a huge +8-10db boost in the entire 4k-10k range. The results can be miraculously positive. Note - This is also an example of how sometimes huge unconventional actions are required to get a great mastering result from a poor mix.
Standard 5-Band Equalizer	Gain	Cut	150hz to 500hz	This is a rarely needed action, but if the bass guitar/synth is very loud and running over everything, you might need to pinpoint it with EQ and *cut* it a bit.
Multi-Band Compressor (GAIN)	Gain	Cut	LOWER-MIDS	Sometimes a 1-2db *cut* in this range will make a song brighter, especially if this BAND is distorted or has no separation. It's addition by subtraction. Subtracting blurry mud leaves brightness.
Multi-Band Compressor (GAIN)	Gain	Cut	LOW Band	If a song mix has super loud bass, *reducing* this BAND a couple dbs will help reduce mud and make it clearer. This range is far from the UPPER-MIDS. So, the bass would have to be very loud to effect them.

Compression	Threshold	Ratio	Location	Notes
Multi-Band Compressor (COMPRESS)	30% to 40%	5:1	LOWER-MIDS	If the LOWER-MIDS are too thick, distorted, vibrating, etc. *compressing* them could improve brightness (because they are running over/disrupting the UPPER-MIDS). This is the "thinning out the band" compression technique.

PROBLEM - NO SPARKLE

Sometimes a song mix is missing that HIGH-end sparkle.

Processor	Control	Action	Location	Notes
Standard 5-Band Equalizer	Gain	Boost	8k-10k Range	A small *boost* between 8k to 10k with a medium Q. Many times this will give you the extra sparkle you need.
Multi-Band Stereo Widener	Widen	Boost w/ Short Delay	HIGH Band	I mentioned this four times already, this is number five! Ha! I love stereo widening the HIGH Band (a medium amount) in every genre. Listen in your headphones. You'll hear how it gives the high-hats a nice subtle stereo spread.

PROBLEM - THIN OR TINNY

A thin song mix is heavier in the UPPER-MIDS and weak in the other BANDS. A tinny song is the same but the problem is more exaggerated.

Your solution is to either *cut* the UPPER-MIDS, or *thicken* and *boost* the volume of the other BANDS (or a combination of both). I've found that *boosting* and *thickening* the areas surrounding the UPPER-MIDS is a better option than *cutting* the tin.

Processor	Control	Action	Location	Notes
Standard 5-Band Equalizer	Gain	Cut	4-6k Range	*Cutting* this offending range down a bit is an option, though usually not very effective as your only remedy. Sometimes I might slightly *cut* it in addition to using some of the thickening techniques below.
Standard 5-Band Equalizer	Gain	Boost	250hz-2k Range, sometimes 6k-8k Range if tinny	*Boosting* around that 250hz-2K range really helps. But if the mixer high pass filtered the vocals and MID level instruments, there might not be too much to boost. A 6k-8k range *boost* might help mask the tin.
Spectral Enhancer	Gain	Boost	LOWER-MIDS, LOW Band	*Enhancing* both of these BANDS will make them thicker which adds warmth and thickness to the entire song. Especially the LOWER-MIDS since they're adjacent to the UPPER-MIDS.
Multi-Band Compressor (GAIN)	Gain	Boost	LOWER-MIDS, LOW Band, HIGH Band	Making the LOWER BANDS *louder* adds thickness. Sometimes the addition of a HIGH Band *boost* will help with tin. You may need to slide the HIGH Band to around 7k.

PROBLEM - VERY BRIGHT

A very bright song mix is one sonic error that sometimes is very difficult to correct.

In audio mastering, it's very easy to brighten up and enhance a dull mix and give it proper tone. This is why you would rather start with a dull mix.

If a mix is very bright (above industry standard), yes (in theory) you can easily cut it down to where it should be, but the problem is the tone won't be right. What you'll be left with is a flat stale master.

Basically, what you want to do in this situation is use my "thin out the band" compression technique then *add* bass thickness/loudness for warmth as needed.

These remedies are similar to the thin/tinny remedies. The difference is, **thin/tinny** needs dramatic LOWER-MID bass *boost*, thickening, and only a slight (if any) brightness *cut*.

Very bright needs a decent amount of brightness *thinned or cut*, while the LOW-end *boost* is less dramatic, since the brightness is being *lowered.*

Processor	Control	Action	Location	Notes
Standard 5-Band Equalizer	Gain	Cut	4k to 6k	You might be able to make a pinpoint EQ *cut* (using a small Q) in efforts to shape your tone a bit. If you *cut* the entire range, you might be left with a lifeless flat sound.
Standard 5-Band Equalizer	Gain	Boost	250hz-1k Range	*Boosting* around that 250hz-1K range really helps. But if the mixer high pass filtered the vocals and MID level instruments, there may not be much to boost.

Spectral Enhancer	Gain	Boost	LOWER-MIDS, LOW Band	*Enhancing* both of these BANDS will make them thicker which adds warmth to the entire song, especially the LOWER-MIDS since they're adjacent to the UPPER-MIDS.
Multi-Band Compressor (Gain)	Gain	Boost	LOWER-MIDS, LOW Band	Making the LOWER BANDS louder adds thickness and helps cover the brightness a bit.
Multi-Band Compressor (Gain)	Gain	Cut	UPPER-MIDS	This is an option, but compression is usually a better one.

Compression	Threshold	Ratio	Location	Notes
Multi-Band Compressor (Compress)	40% to 50%	5:1 to 8:1	UPPER-MIDS	I start my THRESHOLD low (40%) and start *moving up* until the brightness starts to be too much. The logic here is, we're only going to use a *portion* of the UPPER-MIDS, thinning out offending brightness.

IMPORTANT NOTE - If I do thin out the UPPER-MIDS, I still slightly use the **5-Band Standard EQ** and **Spectral Enhancer** to *shape the tone* of the brightness. But not drastic, or it's a counter productive move. If you chop off 1/3 of your UPPER-MIDS and don't adjust the tone, they'll sound flat and lifeless.

PROBLEM - PINCHY (EAR PIERCING) BRIGHT ON LOUD PLAYBACK

I see this problem roughly 5% of the time, and feel it needs to be addressed. After using the compression and EQ techniques (I've previously outlined) in the UPPER-MIDS, sometimes there's still some very pinchy brightness on loud playback. An **EQ cut** in the 5-6k range solves it!

Processor	Control	Action	Location	Notes
Standard 5-Band Equalizer	Gain	Cut	5-6k Range	A -2db to -3db (narrow Q) *cut* in this range will many times eliminate pinchy brightness.

PROBLEM - HI HATS/CYMBALS SUPER BRIGHT OR THICK / TOO MUCH SPARKLE

I mentioned this earlier, but here it is again. A simple volume reduction can solve this problem. I'm not evening listing compression as a solution because I never use it here.

Processor	Control	Action	Location	Notes
Multi-Band Compressor (GAIN)	Gain	Cut	HIGH Band	*Reduce* volume as needed. Slide range to around 7k if needed, to include more of the offending audio in this range. The reverse, obviously if the hats/cymbals aren't loud enough you *boost* volume.

Clarity And Separation (Any BAND)

Clarity and separation is being able to clearly hear all the vocals and instruments. Clarity and separation kind of go hand in hand because if a song mix is crowded and has no separation, it's not going to be very clear. This is more of a *mixing* issue, but there are still a few audio mastering tricks you can do to improve both.

I don't want you to confuse clarity and separation, with brightness and tone. At the same time, a song can be very bright, but not very clear.

DIAGNOSIS AND REMEDY

Some or *all* of the actions given might need to be taken to solve your sonic problem. Decide which processes to use, trial and error with them, and then a little tweaking of the settings will be necessary. What I'm trying to say is, **these aren't blind "set it and forget it" presets.**

PROBLEM - POOR CLARITY

Of course, to solve this problem 100% (and a separation problem) you need to be able to work with each individual track in the mix and create space. But this is mastering. So, you can't 100% solve it, only improve it.

Your only possible options to correct this problem are -

1. Use the **Spectral Enhancer** with its clarity and separation properties (unless the song is already bright enough).

2. *Cut* mud (if there is any) which leaves clarity.

3. Use pinpoint **EQ (5 Band** or **Mid-Side)** to try and bring out the lead vocal, or the lead instrument in an instrumental.

Processor	Control	Action	Location	Notes
Spectral Enhancer	Gain	Boost	UPPER-MIDS	I always try to add at least one unit of spectral enhancing (if possible) to every song for the clarity and separation it brings. In this scenario, you might be able to add a few units.
Multi-Band Compressor (GAIN)	Gain	Cut	LOWER-MIDS	Sometimes a -1db to -2db *cut* in this range will make a song clearer. It's addition by subtraction. Subtracting mud (if there is any) leaves clarity.
Multi-Band Compressor (GAIN)	Gain	Cut	LOW Band	If a song mix has super loud bass, *reducing* this BAND a couple dbs will help reduce mud and make it clearer. This range is far from the UPPER-MIDS. So, the bass would have to be very loud to effect them.
Standard 5-Band Equalizer Or Mid-Side 5-Band Equalizer	Gain	Boost	Various Locations	The trick here is to pull out a narrow Q frequency range, so at least something is more clear and separated (like the lead vocal). This depends on the BAND you're trying to clear up. UPPER-MIDS are for overall song clarity, but maybe you want your kick more clear (*boost* around 80hz), or bass guitar/synth (*boost* around 150hz). Using your **MID-SIDE 5-Band Equalizer** will give you a little more control, since it will allow you to target the inside or outside of the stereo field. Note - Other than a weak stereo field, this might be the only situation where I would use a **MID-SIDE 5-Band Equalizer.** Now that I think of it, another one is when the stereo guitars are super loud and running over everything. You can easily reduce them using EQ on the SIDES *only* (provided they are true stereo panned outside).

Standard 5-Band Equalizer	Gain	Cut	Various Locations	You can also try to cut EQ below the above frequency ranges I mentioned to boost. You're adding clarity by subtracting mud.

Compression	Threshold	Ratio	Location	Notes
Multi-Band Compressor (COMPRESS)	40% to 50%	5:1 to 8:1	LOWER-MIDS	If the LOWER-MIDS are too thick, distorted, vibrating, etc. *compressing* them could improve clarity (because they are running over/disrupting the UPPER-MIDS). This is the "thin the band" compression technique.

PROBLEM - TERRIBLE SEPARATION / MASH OF NOISE / DISTORTION

In this scenario, you could *try* some of the remedies I've given above for "clarity." But if it's really bad, usually your only option is to *thin out* or *eliminate* some of the offending BAND.

Processor	Control	Action	Location	Notes
Multi-Band Compressor (GAIN)	Gain	Cut	Various BANDS	*Lower* the volume of the offending BAND. Heavy compression is a much better option, but this one had to be mentioned.

Compression	Threshold	Ratio	Location	Notes
Multi-Band Compressor (COMPRESS)	40%- 50%	5:1 to 8:1	UPPER-MIDS or LOWER-MIDS	I start my THRESHOLD low (40%) and start *moving up* until the brightness (or distortion) starts to be too much. The logic here is, we're only going to use a *portion* of the BAND, eliminating some of the offending part. Note - You can do this only with ONE BAND. If you need to thin out more than one, you need a remix!
Loudness Maximizer	Threshold	N/A	N/A	Scaling the THRESHOLD down -1db below industry standard will make a song *softer* overall. I very rarely use this option, but if a song is super harsh you need to do something.

IMPORTANT NOTE - If I do thin out the UPPER-MIDS, I still use the **5-Band Standard EQ** and **Spectral Enhancer** to *shape the tone* of the brightness. But not drastic, or it's a counter productive move.

Actually, I combine these actions quite often in the audio mastering process. If you chop off 1/3 of your UPPER-MIDS and don't adjust the tone, they'll sound flat and lifeless.

Bass Volume, Boominess, Kick Punch (Low & Lower Mids)

Bass volume is pretty self-explanatory. You're going to adjust the bass volume as needed using the **Multi-Band Compressor** or **Standard 5-Band EQ**.

When it comes too boominess, a **Spectral Enhancer** can magically *create* bass boominess from a low source, by using harmonics. Of course you can't make bass boominess from *nothing* with this processor, but even with only a small amount, a **Spectral Enhancer** can many times make the bass big and boomy!

DIAGNOSIS AND REMEDY

Some or *all* of the actions given might need to be taken to solve your sonic problem. Decide which processes to use, trial and error with them, and then a little tweaking of the settings will be necessary. What I'm trying to say is, **these aren't blind "set it and forget it" presets.**

PROBLEM - BASS VOLUME IS WRONG

Bass volume is pretty much in the LOW Band, or in the lower part of the LOWER-MIDS.

Processor	Control	Action	Location	Notes
Multi-Band Compressor	Gain	Boost or Cut	LOW Band	*Slide* the LOW Band to the right a bit if you need to get more bass content into the LOW Band. *Boost* or *cut* as needed.
Standard 5-Band Equalizer	Gain	Boost or Cut	150hz (Narrow Q)	If I want to change the volume of the bass guitar/synth *adjust* at around 150hz with a medium Q. Move around to find the sweet spot. The kick is around 80hz.

PROBLEM - BASS NEEDS BOOMINESS

All songs have some boominess. Obviously, hip hop has a ringing boom while hard rock has very little. The **Spectral Enhancer** does a great job adding *boominess* without adding much bass *volume.*

Important Note - Bass volume and boominess are two different sonic characteristics. A lot of times I might need my bass boomier for thickness and presence, but it's already too loud in the mix. When faced with this scenario, I *add* **Spectral Enhancement** in the LOW Band to add boominess, and then *cut* the volume a few dbs with the **Multi-band Compressor** (in the same LOW Band).

I don't think I mention this anywhere else, so remember it. **It's a very common practice in audio mastering to** *reduce* **bass VOLUME, but** *increase* **bass BOOMINESS.** I don't want you to think you shouldn't do this.

Also, there is no way to specifically *remove* boominess. *Reducing* the volume of the LOW Band using the **Multi-band Compressor or 5-Band EQ** is your main remedy.

Processor	Control	Action	Location	Notes
Spectral Enhancer	Gain	Boost	LOW Band	Boost as needed for boominess.

PROBLEM - KICK PUNCH IS WEAK

For some genres, you want the kick to hit hard and cut through the LOW-end. Unfortunately, if the kick in a song mix sounds weak, many times its because the bass guitar/synth wasn't properly high pass filtered and is running the kick over and phasing it out. When this happens, even though the kick was never lowered in the mix, the bass phasing cancels it out so badly, many times you can barely hear it. There is no solution for this other than a remix. But you can try what I suggest below.

If you do suggest a remix for this problem, let the client know they have to high pass EQ filter their bass around 150hz (move a little up if needed) so the kick has its own space. If they try to just raise the volume of a phased out kick, it usually won't work.

Processor	Control	Action	Location	Notes
Multi-Band Compressor (GAIN)	Gain	Boost	LOW Band	If the kick isn't phased out, sometimes this will work.
Standard 5-Band Equalizer	Gain	Boost	80hz to 120hz (Narrow Q)	You can try and boost only the kick drum. In hip hop it will be around 80hz, but could go up to 120hz for classic rock. Watch your EQ meters to see where the kick jumps up in the song to pinpoint the exact frequency.

Warmth, Thickness, Presence (LOWER or UPPER-MIDS)

I call these sonic qualities the fillers. The final pieces of the audio mastering puzzle.

During mastering, I get my (brightness, tone, and sparkle) right first. Then I get my (bass volume and boominess) where it needs to be in relation to the (brightness, tone, and sparkle). **Those are the most important sonic quality combinations in audio mastering.**

Once they are set (warmth, thickness, and presence) are adjusted to compliment them.

DIAGNOSIS AND REMEDY

Some or *all* of the actions given might need to be taken to solve your sonic problem. Decide which processes to use, trial and error with them, and then a little tweaking of the settings will be necessary. What I'm trying to say is, **these aren't blind "set it and forget it" presets.**

PROBLEM - LACK OF WARMTH (HARSHNESS), THICKNESS, PRESENCE

Below are a few techniques I use to add warmth, thickness, presence or reduce harshness in an audio master .

If your goal is *specifically* a warm song (old school rock, jazz, spoken word), make sure you don't initially set your UPPER-MIDS so they're too bright. You might even have to slightly *cut* the brightness in the UPPER-MIDS, in addition to *adding* warmth if a soft analog sound is what you're trying to achieve.

Processor	Control	Action	Location	Notes
Spectral Enhancer	Gain	Boost	LOWER-MIDS and/or LOW Band	*Adding* Spectral Enhancement to the LOWER-MIDS is pure warmth and the first option because it's so close to the UPPER-MIDS. Boominess can also be *added* to the LOW Band, which might also help. This will diminish definition in the LOWER-MIDS a bit, but then again, that's kind of what warmth is. Lack of sharp brightness and clarity.
Multi-Band Compressor (GAIN)	Gain	Boost	LOWER-MIDS and/or LOW Band	*After* **Spectral Enhancement**, a slight +1db to +2db *boost* in these BANDS might also be needed.
Multi-Band	Gain	Cut	UPPER-MIDS	A slight *cut* might be needed to

Compressor (GAIN)				reduce digital brightness. Reducing brightness adds warmth.
Standard 5-Band Equalizer	Gain	Boost	150hz to 500hz	A *boost* anywhere in this range can help add warmth. Try the entire range 300hz-500hz or you could try the 150hz-250hz range, *boosting* the bass guitar/synth. It's all trial and error depending on the mix.
Standard 5-Band Equalizer	Gain	Cut	2k to 6k	A slight EQ *cut* might be in order if you're specifically after a soft analog sound.

De-essing (On song's effects bus)

Check the song for a sharp Sss, Shh, and Chh sounds in the vocals. This is something you definitely do not want in your audio master.

DIAGNOSIS AND REMEDY

PROBLEM - SSS, SHH, AND CHH SOUNDS ARE TOO BRIGHT

If the Sss sound is too bright on the vocal tracks, usually you can use a **De-esser Processor** on the *entire* song and achieve great results. Just make sure it doesn't dull the HIGH-end instruments too much. If it does, request a remix with the vocals de-essed.

HOW TO USE THIS PROCESSOR:

When I use this processor its on the song's effects bus, *not* **on the stereo/main out.** I use a very simple de-esser plug-in that comes with Cubase. It has an auto threshold function that works to perfection. If your de-esser has slightly different settings and you know anything about music processors, it's a no-brainer to figure them out.

1. *Set* THRESHOLD to *auto.*

2. *Set* GENDER as needed.

3. *Set* S-REDUCTION to around -7 (or as needed).

Note - I repeat, I de-ess on the song track effects bus, NOT on the stereo/main out. This way you're effecting the song by itself before other processors on the stereo/main out kick in. This works well for me.

Stereo Width (HIGH Band & UPPER-MIDS w/ Mid-Side EQ)

Stereo width (or lack there of) is most apparent on a car stereo. **When you play your song master in a car, you want it to resonate across the entire stereo spectrum.** You want to hear it from the left door, across the dashboard, all the way to the right door.

When listening to a crappy stereo (mono) song master, it will sound like it's two feet wide right above the car stereo.

Unfortunately, there isn't a real cure in audio mastering for a song mix with a very poor stereo field.

In this section, I'm going to give some options, but they're not very effective.

A remix is the only real solution with some instrumentation and background vocals panned to the outsides.

Client Note - When I request a remix with a better natural stereo field, 90% of the time the client can't do it and uploads basically the same mix. So, it's almost a waste of time to even request it.

I ALWAYS STEREO WIDEN THE HIGH BAND

Using the **Multi-Band Stereo Widener**, I **always** stereo widen the HIGH Band a small amount using a 10ms delay. It's a subtle effect but it gives my song masters a little TOP-end stereo sparkle that sets them apart.

The only exception is if the high hats/cymbals are too loud or thick. In this case, stereo widening would cause them to be over powering and very annoying. I don't want that.

DIAGNOSIS AND REMEDY

PROBLEM - STEREO FIELD IS TOO NARROW

A. I use the **Mid-Side EQ** in the UPPER-MIDS.
B. *Set* it to SIDE. Very important - **SIDE ONLY.**
C. EQ *boost* (3-5k Range).

Unfortunately, if a song is weak in the stereo field to begin with, there won't be *much* to boost on the sides. Usually just light stereo reverb. But you don't have many other options.

ALTERNATE REMEDY - You could also use a **Single-Band Stereo Widener** (on the song's track bus). I rarely use this effect because it eventually starts widening the center of the mix, but it is an option. This is an extra optional processor. I didn't even mention it in my audio mastering processors section because it isn't used enough.

Overall Volume

To determine song average volume levels (so I can match and balance them), I use EZ CD Audio Converter which has ReplayGain as a function. It costs only around $40.

Get a 30 day FREE demo of the software here - http://SongVolume.com

I saw some dude online selling a volume analyzer for over $100. I don't know if his even works, but you don't need it. **ReplayGain** has undisputed accuracy, and is the only volume analyzer you'll EVER need. If you've never heard of this software, this tip alone is worth several times the price of this book!

How does it work? **ReplayGain** uses an algorithm to measure the overall average *perceived* loudness of a song (or any audio data). And it's *very* accurate!

A standard peak meter tells you the loudest part of a song, which is worthless for balancing song volumes. Most of my clients are pretty sharp when it comes to a song's sonic qualities. Well, when I use **ReplayGain** to match and balance song volumes for them it's hardly ever contested. A client might question the volume level on maybe 1 out of every 50 songs I master, and even then they're probably wrong. It's that good!

Here Are The Industry Standard ReplayGain Volume Settings I've Used On Over 30,000 Songs

96 - This is the *lowest* I'll go, and only if a client *demands* it. Any lower and they'll be back a week later complaining for a refund because it's not loud enough.

97 - Old School Rock, Jazz, Classical, Most Movie Soundtracks, Kids Songs, Spoken Word.

98-98.5 - Pop, Dance, EDM, Pop Rock, Country, R&B, Reggae, Alternative.

99-99.5 - Hip Hop, Rap, Hard Rock, Heavy Metal.

100 - This is the *max* I will ever go, and only if a client requests it. And, I can get there without distorting.

101-102 - This is as loud as you can mathematically go. I've never heard a commercial song louder than 101.5 (though I haven't checked every song on the radio either). And many times these super loud masters don't sound very good.

Note - Even using a good loudness maximizer, its tough to go over 100 and not distort or start pumping. The good news is, you don't have to.

I see a lot of people *obsessed* with loudness and will try to go 101-102. **All you're doing is ruining your song when the loudest songs on commercial radio are at roughly 100 max.**

HERE ARE A FEW IMPORTANT NOTES ON LOUDNESS MAXIMIZATION

1. There's a half db variance on some of the volume settings I give. **Whenever possible I will use the higher one.** This decision is based on how the song sounds. If the higher setting doesn't have enough dynamic range or I don't like the extra saturation, I won't use it.

Studio Tip - If you're running an online recording studio, a little louder is better. You don't want to get beaten out by the competition *only* because their master is +1/2 db louder than yours.

And if you're someone who doesn't double check their final song volumes and gives out previews -2dbs or more below industry standard, you'll NEVER get any work online!

2. Sometimes you're trying to loudness maximize a song, but you can't match the ReplayGain number. Or you get to the number but the song is distorted. Here's one solution that usually works. *Compress* the LOWER-MIDS and UPPER-MIDS *hard*. "Cut the top off" and *lower* the THRESHOLD on both, and then you can *raise* the **Loudness Maximizer.**

Remember, you have to use your ears here. You can't just blindly super compress your BANDS and then loudness maximize a crazy amount. You'll either badly distort or you'll have a heavy saturated mash of noise. Move your THRESHOLD down little by little until you get it right. Don't just drop it down to 50% right off the bat and destroy the song.

I rarely use this technique. It's very rarely ever needed. Your standard compression and loudness maximization will get you to industry standard volume 99% of the time.

3. The more volume you add with a Loudness Maximizer, the more *harshness* you add. This isn't necessarily a bad thing. But if someone wants a very soft master, *lowering* the THRESHOLD even an extra -1/2db below industry standard will make the master softer.

I also do this when a song mix is a total mash of noise (and it can't be improved). It's so thick and crappy, an extra -1/2db lower in volume helps.

4. **When trying to determine a song's average volume level, be sure to include the loudest part of the song in your export.** If a song's dynamic range is +5dbs or less, you should get a very accurate average volume reading. If your dynamic range is +6db or more, the next sections explain how to deal with this problem.

VERY IMPORTANT - WHAT IF THE VOLUME OF A FEW SONG SECTIONS ARE ERRATIC (TOO DYNAMIC)?

By erratic song sections I mean the chorus is +10dbs louder than the verses, and +5dbs louder than the bridge, etc. Anything +6dbs or more, could (but not always) give you a false **ReplayGain** reading. A +10db difference guaranteed will.

When it comes to an overall volume reading, everything revolves around the loudest part of the song.

When I want to check the average volume level of a very erratic (too dynamic) song, **I set my locators *ONLY* on the loudest section and export *ONLY* that small section.** My volume level assessments are based *only* on the loudest section of the song.

If I were to use the entire song for assessment, I WILL get a false average volume reading. If I loudness maximize using these false readings, and the loudest parts of the song will distort. Working with and exporting only the loudest section of the song eliminates this problem.

And of course, *never* export only the lower volume sections of a song (which defies common logic). That will obviously give you a false reading and distortion.

On the flip side, if a song has +5dbs or less of dynamic range, set your locators to include at least one verse and the loudest part of the song and you will get a spot on average volume reading.

COMPRESSION MADE EASY

Since compression is such a big part of audio mastering it has its own separate section.

Add a little bass or treble, even a child knows the basics of EQ. But when it comes to compression, many audio engineers who own a recording studio, or work in one for a living, don't understand it very well. I know this by the number of re-master jobs I receive from studios all around the world that don't apply *any* compression at all!

After reading this section, you'll know everything you need to about compression in audio mastering.

Which Compressors Are Used In Audio Mastering?

Before I get into what compressors can do in audio mastering, I have to mention which two I use.

1. Loudness Maximizer - Is used to raise the overall volume level of a song to industry standard level, without distorting.

2. A Multi-Band Compressor - Has several functions that I explain in the next section.

Important Note - From here on out in this book, when I mention COMPRESSION I am referring to actual compressing, limiting, squeezing an audio track.

If I mention GAIN, I'm referring to a volume level increase using the **Multi-Band Compressor**. YES, in addition to compressing, you can increase or reduce the volume level of a BAND with a **Multi-Band Compressor**.

What Can Compressors Do In Audio Mastering?

A lot of sound engineers think all compressors are used for is limiting / squeezing / compressing an audio signal (which you could also call reducing volume spikes). Yes, a compressor can do this, but there are a few other reasons why a compressor is used.

THRESHOLD AND RATIOS SETTINGS

Let me first briefly explain these two settings. (I get into more detail with graphics later in the book.)

The **THRESHOLD** setting determines *when* the compressor turns on and off. Just like a thermostat determines when a furnace turns on and off.

The **RATIO** setting determines the *amplitude* (heavy, moderate, slight, etc.) of compression. Ratio examples would be 1 to 1 (OFF), 2 to 1 (light), 8 to 1 (heavy), 30 to 1 (extreme limiting).

The **RATIO** setting *only* affects audio that passes the **THRESHOLD**.

Any audio content *above* the THRESHOLD is affected by the RATIO setting. Any audio content *below* the THRESHOLD is not affected.

If you set your **THRESHOLD** so high that the compressor never turns on, obviously your **RATIO** setting is irrelevant. This would be like setting an alarm clock for 6am, but the alarm is turned off. The alarm time is worthless because it won't go off.

Also, if your **RATIO** is 1/1, this means it's OFF. In this case, the **THRESHOLD** setting is irrelevant because no matter where you set it, you didn't set a compression amount.

To recap, the **THRESHOLD** setting is *when* the compressor turns on and how much of the audio signal is affected. The **RATIO** setting is the *amplitude* (the degree) of compression.

WHAT A MULTI-BAND COMPRESSOR CAN DO IN AUDIO MASTERING

A Compressor Can Reduce Volume Spikes

This is done by reducing an audio track's volume level once it passes a set *threshold*.

A Compressor Can Reduce Dynamic Range

Reducing dynamic range is actually a by-product of reducing volume spikes (the previous paragraph). The more you reduce the volume spikes, the less dynamic range the audio track has because you are bringing the loudest parts of the audio track closer to the quietest parts.

The article in the next section, "Why Would You Want Less Dynamic Range" gives more details on this subject.

A Compressor Can Make A Song Sound More Cohesive

You record the vocals, bass guitar, lead guitar, etc. sometimes all on different days, maybe even in different studios. Using the **Multi-Band Compressor** is the main process in audio mastering that helps make a song mix sound like everyone is playing together, not a bunch of separate tracks.

When you apply the proper amount of compression to each of the four BANDS, it's hard to explain without hearing it, but the song sounds tighter, more together. Sometimes the effect is subtle, but when you do an A/B comparison between the properly mastered song and the unmastered uncompressed song mix, you *will* hear a positive difference. The song is more cohesive.

It Can Properly Balance The Volume Levels Between The Four Bands

You can use the GAIN function to adjust the BAND volume levels as needed. This allows you to balance the volume levels of the four BANDS against each other.

Not to add any confusion, but this is considered EQ. Most understand compression to only be the act of squeezing, limiting, lowering, compressing, etc. an audio track.

But if I were to *gain* the LOW Band +5dbs, I'm making the LOW Band frequency range *louder* which is an equalization process.

A Compressor Is An EQ Cutter

A **Muti-Band Compressor** can also be used as an EQ *cutter*. Notice as you *lower* the THRESHOLD in the UPPER-MIDS, the brightness decreases (provided you have a RATIO of at least 2:1 set). The volume of the entire BAND decreases as you *lower* the THRESHOLD. This is an EQ *cut*.

A Compressor Can Thin Out A Band

If the audio content in a BAND is too thick, harsh, distorted, vibrates, etc. a compressor can thin it out using the correct THRESHOLD/RATIO combination. I get into this topic in detail later in the book.

A Compressor Can Make A Song Louder Without It Distorting

Yes, a **Loudness Maximizer** (not the Multi-band Compressor) is what you use to make a song as loud as the commercial songs on the radio, without distorting.

Working With A Compressor's Threshold And Ratio Settings

I've mastered over 30,000 songs to amazing sound quality, **and I've learned that *THRESHOLD* and *RATIO* are by far your most important settings when working with compression.** For all other functions/settings, I just use whatever is on my initial preset template.

One reason is because when you compress an entire song, the compressor doesn't turn on and off as when compressing an individual track. So, attack and release settings aren't that important.

Now, *some* compressors do have tube, warm, tape, etc. settings that will give you a different tone, and a hard/light compression knee. These are simple self-explanatory functions. Use them on a trial and error basis as you see fit. I usually use a tube setting, but if it's old school rock, jazz, R&B I might use warm.

The hard/light knee setting helps if you have a part in a song that jumps out real loud. If you find this part distorts or crackles, a light knee setting might correct this problem. This light setting is rarely ever needed if you use an accurate average volume meter reading and don't over-maximize.

Important Note - I might touch on hardware compressors a bit, but this section is written mainly for digital software multi-band compressor for two reasons.

1. At least 75% (if not more) of the people reading this book are going to use software compressors.

2. For educational purposes, It's MUCH easier for the reader to know exactly where their settings should be if they can *see* the .wav file on the compressor's digital readout. They'll also be able to see *how* the compressor affects the .wav file, which is a great learning experience.

You can still use all of my combinations with a hardware compressor, its just a little harder for a beginner because hardware metering is not as detailed (sometimes just a row of light bulbs going up and down). A lot is done by ear.

If you're just starting out, I highly recommend using multi-band compression *software*, if *only* for the learning experience. Buy it or use the free stock compressor software that comes with your DAW software, so you can *SEE* what compression settings do to the signal (.wav file). **http://BestMasteringSoftware.com** is a great choice.

THRESHOLD AND RATIO COMBINATION POSSIBILITIES

There are roughly 3,900 legitimate possible threshold and ratio combinations, but I'm going to reduce this by 95%, making the entire compression process MUCH easier! **That *is* an audio mastering "secret!"**

I say, "legitimate" possible combinations because many combinations cannot be used. Like *thresholds* of 30% or lower (with a higher ratio), or *ratios* lower than 2:1 (which is basically off).

I pretty much use only four different *threshold* positions and six different *ratio* settings. **That reduces your combination possibilities from 3,900 down to only 24!**

Compression THRESHOLD and RATIO Settings

I was going to get into the science of thresholds and ratios, but it's really not needed. **You will be able to achieve your goals without it.**

THRESHOLD SETTINGS

The THRESHOLD setting determines *when* the compressor turns on and off, and *how much* of the audio signal is compressed (reduced/limited).

I work in percentages when dealing with THRESHOLD settings.

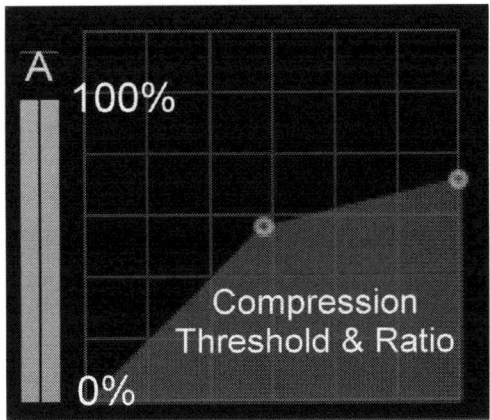

In this compressor meter photo, A is your peak meter (this photo is a Cubase compressor).

If you were to set your *threshold* equal to the highest volume peak of a song (100%), the compressor will NEVER go on. On the flip side, if you set your *threshold* at the very bottom (0%) of the song volume level (with a high ratio), it will completely compress and eliminate the audio signal. You won't be able to hear anything.

Let me explain this a different way. First I have to go back to my dynamic range definition.

As a song plays, the output meter constantly goes up and down. **Dynamic range is the area between the peak level (when the meter is up, 100%) and the low level (when the meter is down, 0%).** This dynamic range is what's affected by compression, and the *threshold* setting determines *how much* of it (what percentage) is effected.

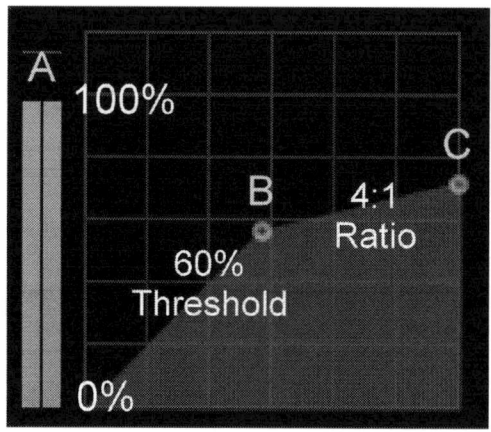

In this photo A is your peak meter, B is your threshold, the line between B and C is your ratio amplitude (set at 4 to 1). If you were brickwall limiting (30 to 1 or infinity) the line between B and C would be a straight line.

Any time I refer to a *threshold* setting, I do it in percentages. If I tell you to set your *threshold* at 60%, you're setting it 40% below the audio's top peak volume level of 100%. If I say 50%, you're setting it right in the middle of the audio content.

Of course, you will need to be using a software compressor to be able to *see* the audio content for exact *threshold* setting placement. If you're using hardware, metering is more vague, but you can still do it.

HOW MUCH OF THE SIGNAL IS COMPRESSED?

Now, this is the part many people don't understand about compression. Where ever you set your *threshold,* anything ABOVE it is the only thing that's compressed!

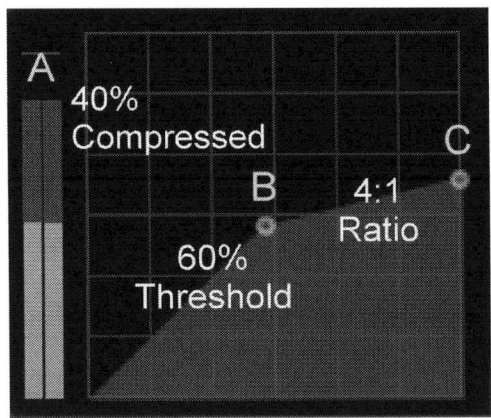

Back to the 60% threshold example. The 40% range above the THRESHOLD is the *only* part of the audio that is compressed. Anything *below* the THRESHOLD setting is left *untouched.*

And your RATIO setting determines *how much* of it is compressed. If your RATIO is at 1 to 1 (off), nothing is compressed. If its set at 30 to 1, you're brickwall limiting and cutting off (eliminating) the entire top 40% of the audio peak (loudest part of the song). In the photo above, the ratio is 4 to 1.

WHY DO I WORK IN PERCENTAGES?

I can't tell you to set your *thresholds* in dbs because song mix volumes can greatly vary.

For example, if I told you to set your *threshold* at -3dbs and a song mix peaks at 0 meter level, then you would be compressing the top 3dbs of the song mix.

But what if the song mix peaks at -6dbs under 0 level? Using a *threshold* setting of -3dbs, the compressor would never even turn on. Not even close!

Now, if I told you to set your *threshold* at 80%, this would work with ANY song mix. You'd be compressing the top 20% of any song regardless of its overall volume, because your *threshold* setting is relative to the song's peak volume level, not a 0 meter level.

RATIO SETTINGS

The compression RATIO setting determines the *amplitude* (heavy, average, slight, etc) of the compression. Only audio ABOVE the *threshold* is affected by this RATIO.

Here Are The Threshold And Ratio Setting I Use In Audio Mastering

---

MY THRESHOLD SETTINGS

I only use four basic positions.

80% HIGH - Just below the very top of the .wav file peak.

65% HIGH-MID RANGE

50% MID-RANGE - In the middle of the .wav file.

40% BELOW MID-RANGE

MY RATIO SETTINGS

I only use six basic compression ratios.

2 to 1 RATIO - Extremely Light

3 to 1 RATIO - Very Light

4 to 1 RATIO - Slight

5 to 1 RATIO - Average

8 to 1 RATIO - Heavy

30 to 1 RATIO (Infinity) - Brickwall Limiting

Compression Threshold/Ratio Combinations

Below are a few *threshold* graphic examples using Izotope Ozone, **BestMasteringSoftware.com**

Using a software like this, it's easy to see where the .wav peaks (100%), the middle of the .wav (50%) and the very bottom (0%), making your *threshold* decisions basically a no-brainer. This gives you a good compression starting point. And then A/B compare and tweak your settings using your ears. A very easy process!

Important Note - The earlier compressor meter photos are from the program Cubase. The peak meter on Cubase goes up and down, the same way a hardware compressor peak meter does. The problem with these meters is you can see **where** the meter peaks, but you can't see **how thick** the song is. Is it a thin hi-hat that's peaking in the song, or an orchestra blast? Both could look exactly the same on this meter.

In the Ozone compressor photo below (in the left column), you can also see the *thickness* of the song. The few little tiny lines at the top are thin audio content and can be eliminated (cut the top off).

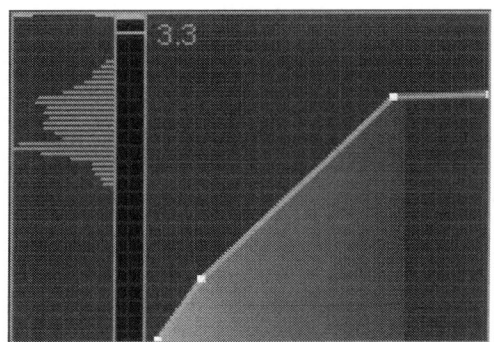

Why is this important? Because the thinner the peak, the more you can compress it. For example, the top 20% of your song could be very thin audio content that can be compressed (eliminated) with no negative consequences.

But if the top 20% is thick audio content, you might not be able to cut much of it off, if any. You can't tell this using the Cubase or a hardware compressor peak meter. You can with Ozone.

Here are a few of the most common used *threshold/ratio* combinations, so you can see how they look and affect the .wav file.

No Compression

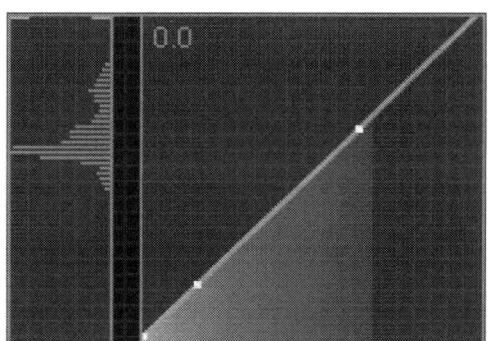

This example shows no compression. **The RATIO is (1:1) which basically means off.** The THRESHOLD is at 50% but no matter what you set it at, the compressor won't do anything because of there's no RATIO.

Slight Compression Amount

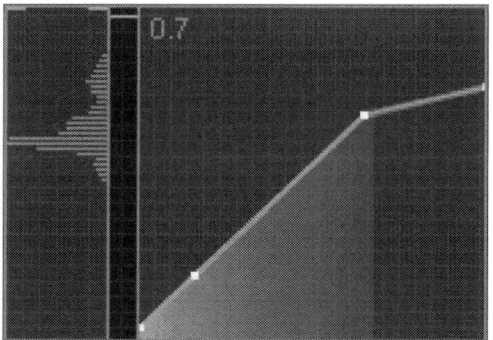

I start EVERY band with *slight compression*. Many times that's all you need in the LOW, HIGH and LOWER-MID BANDS. **The settings shown are THRESHOLD 50% and RATIO (4:1).**

Note - My *slight compression* settings will vary by BAND. More in the section "Initial Template Setup."

Cut The Top Off

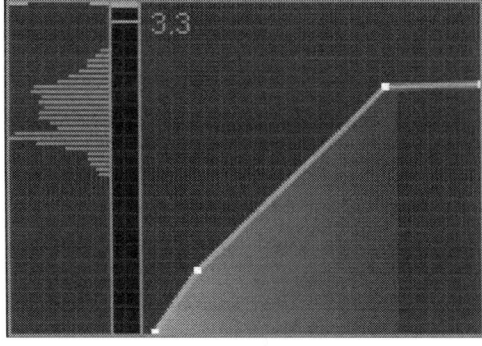

This is basically brickwall limiting the very peak of a song (just when it starts breaking up) in the UPPER-MIDS. Of course if you need to set the *threshold* lower to achieve this goal, do it. This setting is just a basic example. **The settings above are THRESHOLD 80% and RATIO (30:1).**

Thinning Out The Band Out

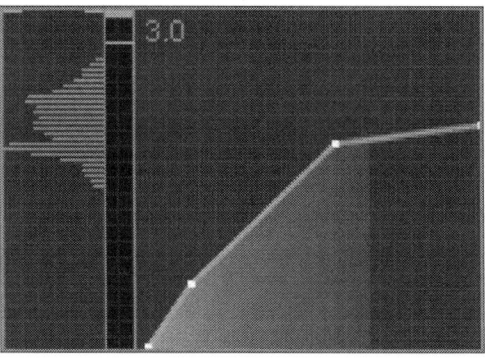

Sometimes a BAND is just too thick or distorted and needs thinning out. There are two ways to do this. Higher *threshold* (40%) and high *ratio* (8:1), or lower *threshold* (30%) and a lower *ratio* (3:1). **Higher *threshold* (40%) and High *ratio* (8:1) is the common approach and what's shown above.**

How A Compressor Affects A .Wav File

This was a last minute addition to the book, but a very important one! I want to show a side-by-side comparison of exactly what a compressor does.

In the photo below, the top .wav file is what you might receive from a client.

The bottom .wav, is after compression. I "cut the top off" in the UPPER-MIDS using a *threshold* of 80% and a *ratio* of 30-1 (or you might have infinity as your brickwall limiting setting).

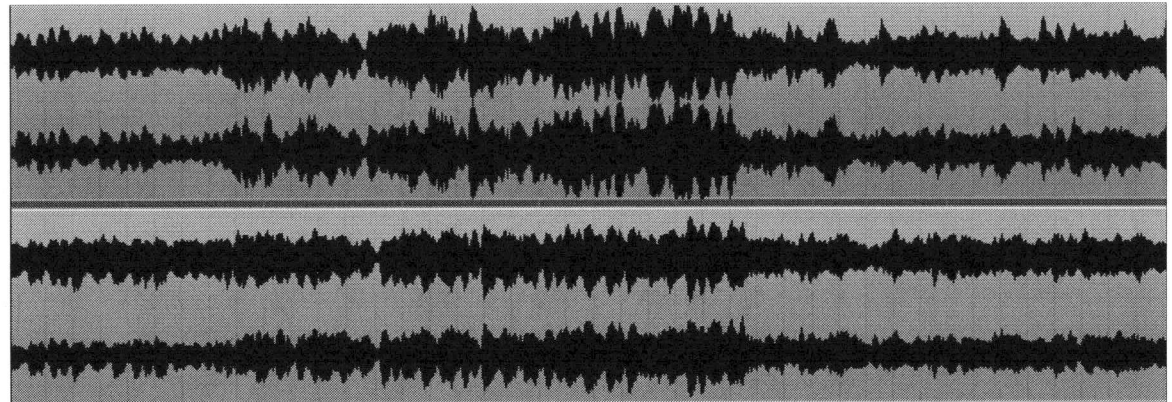

Notice how the results are as expected. Comparing the two files, roughly 20% of the highest peaks are cut off, and everything else is pretty much left untouched. The compressor was set to do this, and looking at the .wav files, the goal was achieved!

This photo is an overlap of the two photos above. The loudest black peaks are being eliminated by the compressor.

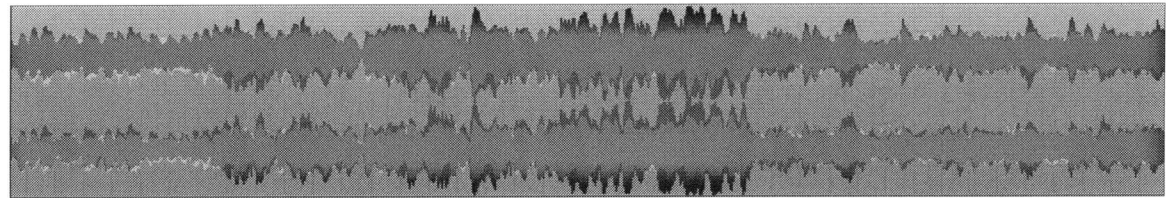

WHY CAN'T YOU HEAVY COMPRESS AN ERRATIC SECTION SONG AS A REMEDY?

If you have a song that's 10dbs louder in the choruses compared to the verses, yes you *can* "cut the top off" with compression using a 40% *threshold*. Visually the file will *look* great, and the huge dynamic range will be gone.

The problem is when you listen to it! The previously loud choruses will guaranteed be TOTALLY muffled. Even a client that doesn't know much about music will reject it.

You can't use compression to bring down the loud parts. You have to either *gain* the loud sections *down*, or *gain* the lowest volume sections *up*.

Note - In this section, when I refer to GAIN, I'm talking about highlighting the file with your cursor and using your DAW software's GAIN function to change the volume.

What Are Your Compression Goals By BAND?

In this section I'm going to discuss compression goals and a few actions for each BAND. I'm going to try and keep this as simple as possible (and it is all quite simple).

I might touch on a few of these details again in the "Audio Mastering Step-By-Step" section, but *this* section will have the most information on the subject. **So be sure to read it!**

During the audio mastering process, I do take the entire song as a whole into consideration but my *main focus* is on each individual BAND. I have compression goals for each of the four BANDS and once they are achieved the entire song as a whole is properly compressed.

LOW AND HIGH BANDS

I will start out with the LOW and HIGH Bands because they're very easy to work with.

I apply *slight compression* to the LOW and HIGH Bands using the Multi-Band Compressor. 90% of the time this is the *only compression* I apply to these BANDS. But, I do often use the **Multi-Band Compressor's** GAIN function for volume control.

The LOW Band - I almost always need to *boost* or *cut* the volume 1-2 dbs (sometimes more).

The HIGH Band - You need to get the hi hat/cymbal volume just right so it's loud enough to drive the music, but not annoying or hissy.

If I do adjust the volume in the HIGH Band using the GAIN function, I always slide the range left (to around 7k) to include more of the hi hat/cymbals combo. Keep sliding left until you get what you need in the BAND.

UPPER-MIDS

The UPPER-MIDS is where a song's brightness and clarity resides. It's also where a song breaks up if played loud. Most of your music and vocal content resides here too. **This is why the UPPER-MIDS are the main focus in audio mastering.**

I have a few compression goals for this BAND and I *try* to achieve ALL of them. I might have to compensate between a few of the goals, and a very poor mix will make some of these goals impossible, but I still *try* to achieve *all of them.*

A. I want to keep everything as natural as possible. If *NO* compression achieves my compression goals (matches the reference track, sounds good, etc) I'm not adding any. Many times genres like Rock only require slight compression in every BAND because Rock engineers usually compress their mixes very well.

B. I want to retain as much dynamic range as possible, so that it doesn't sound smashed.

C. I want to retain the proper brightness level. Sometimes a mix already has close to the perfect amount of brightness. I don't want to improperly reduce this with compression, and then have to boost the brightness back up later (this would be one of those counter productive actions I talk about).

D. I want the UPPER-MIDS to be the proper volume level in relation to the song. It has to sit right in the mix.

E. I don't want them sounding too thick or distorted, or thinning out the BAND might be needed.

F. And lastly, I don't want the UPPER-MIDS breaking up on loud playback.

HOW DO YOU KNOW WHEN COMPRESSION IS GOOD IN THE UPPER-MIDS?

First, by looking at the song mix .wav. You can kind of tell how much overall compression it already has. If it's a non-dynamic straight line, only a *slight* amount of compression (if any) is needed.

When its time to set my *final* compression level in the UPPER-MIDS, I monitor the song loud (100-105dbs).

I start my **Muti-Band Compressor** THRESHOLD at around 40% with a 5:1 RATIO and start *sliding* (or turning the knob) of the THRESHOLD *up*. I keep going *up* until the song starts breaking up or burning my ears. Once this happens, I move the THRESHOLD back *down* a bit.

I then tweak the RATIO. I try 3:1 but maybe I need to go to 30 to 1 (infinity brickwall) to achieve my goal of the song not breaking up. And then another slight THRESHOLD tweak might be needed.

I guess the answer to the question is -

1. When the UPPER-MIDS no longer break up.

2. And, when you also did your best trying to achieve all of the goals mentioned above.

With a hardware compressor, it's basically the same concept but I apply the THRESHOLD actions in reverse.

First, I set my RATIO, and then I start my THRESHOLD at the very *top* setting (so the compressor is off). I then start working the THRESHOLD *down* until the song stops breaking up.

LOWER-MIDS

In the LOWER-MIDS, *most* of the time this frequency BAND only requires slight compression, unless its problematic (too thick, harsh, or vibrates). I address how to fix this problem later in the book.

There are other actions more commonly taken in this BAND, it's just that compression isn't usually one of them.

The Power Of Thinning Out A Band

This isn't a ground breaking concept, but I use this compression technique so often to correct errors, I had to repeat it and give it its own section.

Here are the common errors I see in each BAND, which can be improved by BAND thinning:

UPPER-MIDS - Super bright, Distorted, Very Thick/Total Saturation (a mash of noise).

LOWER-MIDS - Distorted, Vibrating, Very Thick With No Clarity (a big muffle).

HIGH Band & LOW Band - I *rarely ever* thin out these BANDS. If they're problematic, volume adjustment is my chosen solution.

HOW BAND THINNING WORKS

When it comes to problematic UPPER-MIDS and LOWER-MIDS the logic here is **you're trying to eliminate a large PORTION of the problematic BAND by using the Multi-Band Compressor.** You could say I'm trying to cut it in half.

Using *all* the audio content in a problematic BAND isn't going to work. But if I use a THRESHOLD setting of 60% and a RATIO of 8:1, I'm eliminating roughly 40% of the offending BAND. And many times the remaining audio content blends nicely into the song mix.

How do you know how much to compress when thinning? I start my THRESHOLD at around 40% with a RATIO of 8:1 and start moving the THRESHOLD *up* (45%, 50%, 55%, etc). Once the offending material becomes too problematic, I *stop* moving up and pull back *down* a bit. Then a slight RATIO tweak and I'm done.

You can also try a **LOWER** THRESHOLD (30%) and **LOWER** RATIO (3:1) to thin out the BAND. See if that solves your problem better than the previous settings.

*** VIDEO EXAMPLE ***

HOW TO THIN OUT A BAND

http://audiomasteringsecrets.com/thin.html

Note - **This technique works well if you have only *one* poor BAND.** If your LOW Band, LOWER-MIDS and UPPER-MIDS are ALL terrible, you can't just cut them all in half! Ha! It won't work.

VERY IMPORTANT NOTE - After thinning out the UPPER-MIDS, I *still* might use the **5-Band Standard EQ** and **Spectral Enhancer** to shape the *tone* of the brightness. Actually, I do this on *most* of the songs I work on, if even a slight amount.

Many times, if you chop off 1/3 or more of your UPPER-MIDS, and don't adjust the brightness tone, they'll sound flat and lifeless.

Why Would You Want Less Dynamic Range?

From an audio mastering standpoint, **less dynamic range means you can make the overall volume of a song louder.**

Another reason is if your song section volumes are erratic (too dynamic). For example, the chorus is +10dbs louder than the verses. Reducing dynamic range would bring their volume levels closer together.

If you're trying to reduce a song's dynamic range and make its overall volume level louder (which is loudness maximization), the good news is this specific audio mastering compression process is taken care of by the **Loudness Maximizer** program, and is basically a no-brainer. You set the *threshold* to get as much overall volume as needed and the program does the rest.

Note - A **Loudness Maximizer** *can* distort. Once you achieve your desired loudness, you have to actually *listen* to the song closely to make sure it's not distorting (not just *look* at the .wav file). Let your ears be the judge.

Compression Mostly Affects The Loudest Parts Of A Song

I felt this was a completely obvious concept, but then again I realized if a reader doesn't know this it would create major problems. So here we go!

If you start your THRESHOLD at 100% (at the highest peak of the song) and move down to say 80%, only 20% of the song will be compressed (at the RATIO you set). We've already talked about this. **But this pertains only to the LOUDEST PART of the song.**

Why do you need to know this? What if the chorus in a song is +10dbs louder than the verses? If you set your THRESHOLD at 80%, the compressor will do NOTHING to the verses. It can't. It isn't set low enough to even turn on when the verses are playing because they're not loud enough.

I'm not saying you *need* to specifically compress your verses. This was just an example of how only the loudest section of this song was being compressed.

You *can* independently compress different frequency BANDS. But you *cannot* independently compress *each section* of a song, especially if their volume levels are far apart. The loudest part gets compressed first, and as you go down with your THRESHOLD more of the lower volume parts are compressed.

I had to bring this photo back. The second photo is compressed, the first photo is not. **Notice how the loudest parts of the .wav file are affected the most.** The lower volume parts, very little if at all.

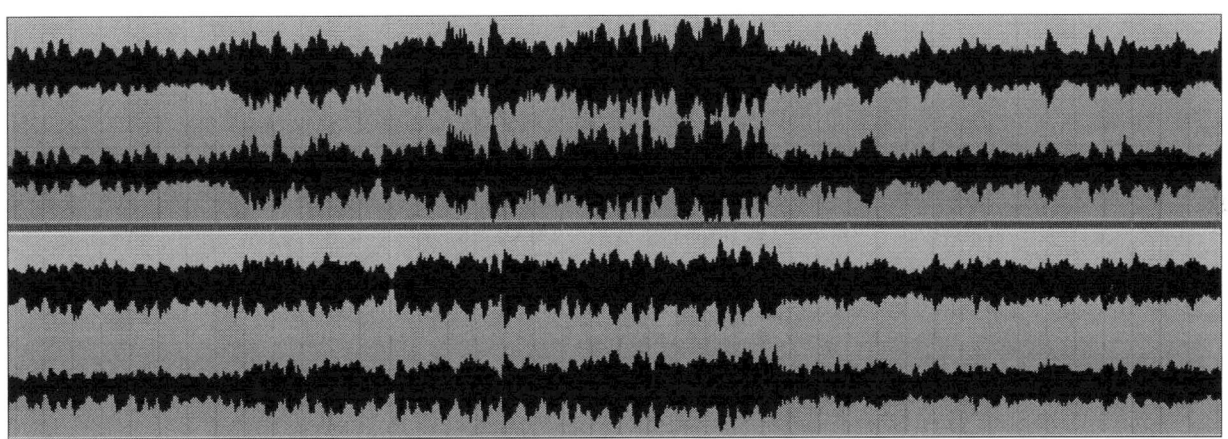

ALL YOU NEED TO FOCUS ON IS THE LOUDEST PARTS

Another very important audio mastering fact is that since compression is peak reduction, **once you've properly compressed the loudest parts, your compression on the song is done!**

You don't even have to consider the lower volume sections. The lower sections can't possibly peak too loud because they're underneath the louder sections you already properly compressed.

Its kind of like cutting some wild grass that has 6, 4, and 2 inch patches. If you set the lawn mower at 2.5 inches and cut the entire lawn, you're done. The grass is now all within 1/2 inch, most of it at 2.5 inches. You don't have to go back and address the 2 inch patches.

Note - **This only works with compression.** You can't just correct the brightest or bass level of ONE *section* of a song and the whole rest of the song is good to go. Sometimes the verses are at a low volume level but are brighter than the choruses. Kind of rare, but it happens.

Why Do I Never Remove Compression As A Remedy?

In this book, when I diagnose and give remedies for song mix problems, I never tell you to *remove* compression. The simple reason why is because I always start each project with only a very slight amount of compression on each BAND. **You're basically starting every song with the compression already off!** There's no need for me to tell you to remove it.

The only time you would remove compression is if *you* applied too much during mastering and need to scale it back.

AUDIO MASTERING PROCEDURES

Here are several audio mastering procedures you need to remember when working on your projects.

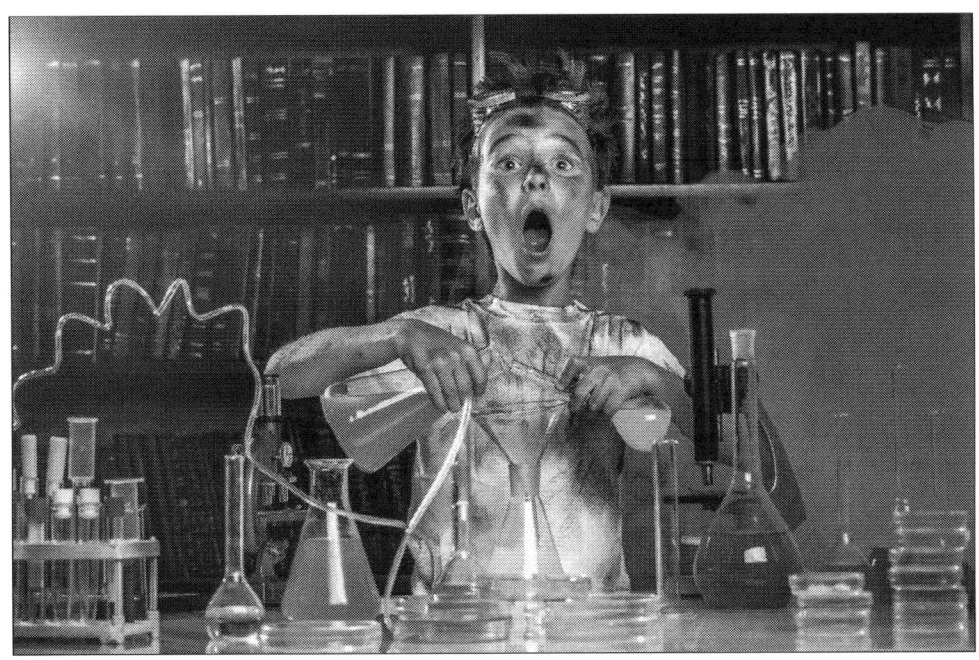

Should You Export Your Mix To .WAV Or Mix And Master At The Same Time?

Myself, I mix and master at the same time. Effects are applied to all the individual tracks *and* the stereo/main out at the same time. If you're mastering and mixing a project, you have the option to do it like this too.

Now, if a friend or client gives you a stereo .wav file of a song, obviously you only have one option because you're only doing the mastering.

What should YOU do, If you're mixing *and* mastering a project?

I HIGHLY recommend that you export your mix as a stereo .wav file (at least a few times even if you're a pro at mixing). Then import this file into a mastering project session.

This book is written from that viewpoint. You start with a stereo .wav file song mix, analyze it, and then apply the proper mastering effects.

This is a mastering book, and that's where I'm keeping its focus. Mastering a single stereo .wav file. When you have a *great* understanding of this, then you can mix and master at the same time, like I do.

If I wrote this book from the viewpoint of "mixing and mastering" at the same time, there would be mass confusion concerning where the corrective actions should be taken. In mixing or mastering?

Note – I understand you might be mastering a .aiff file or maybe an mp3. To keep it simple, I always refer to a song mix file as a .wav.

But What If The Mix Is Terrible, Shouldn't You Fix It?

YES! A lot of fixes can't be done in mastering. For example, if the vocals are way too low in volume and need to be raised, this can't be fixed in audio mastering. If you have access to the raw mix, by all means fix it. And export a new .wav file.

Also "after" mastering, the fact alone that the song is much louder reveals unknown problems in the mix that might need to be corrected.

The Importance of Good A/B Comparison And Mix Evaluation

In a future section, I explain step-by-step how I master a song. But even though I cover this, if you're poor at A/B comparison and mix evaluation, you won't be able to master songs very well.

Here's a simple example why:

Song A is a commercial reference track. Song B is the .wav file you're mastering. In terms of *brightness*, let's say they are **exactly** the same. My sonic quality remedy section tells you what to do if a song mix is too bright, or not bright enough compared to the commercial reference track.

In this scenario, we know both songs are *equal* in terms of brightness. The mix already matches the reference track. So, we do **NOTHING** for the brightness sonic quality.

Here's where a problem could arise. Let's say after making your song B mix evaluation, you *think* its very dull compared to the reference song A. *You're wrong*, but this is what you *think* because you're poor at A/B comparison and mix evaluation.

Because you *think* the mix is dull, you're going to use the steps I outline on how to make a song mix brighter, and now your master is too bright. **You shouldn't have applied any brightening effects since the song mix already matched the reference track in terms of brightness.**

In this book, I give you the exact steps I take in the mastering process, my laws of audio master, audio mastering concepts, and even sonic quality tips for each genre, but **if you can't A/B compare and match a reference track, all this information is worthless.** You won't be able to properly master music.

Good A/B comparison and matching reference tracks comes with practice. The more you work at it, the better you'll get.

And feedback from people knowledgeable in music will help you know how good your matching abilities and mastering skills are.

Getting Your Songs To Translate Well on Different Mediums

Your main music mediums are a car stereo, earphones or headphones, smaller to medium sized powered stereo speakers, and maybe a desktop computer or laptop. These are the most popular. Also, a lot of my music is played on big systems in dance clubs by DJs. That's another one.

I've been doing this for *many* years and I can tell you from experience, if you learn your studio speaker setup very well, and make a great master, it will sound great on ALL mediums mentioned above. All of them!

At this point in my career, I can do it like this because I know my studio speaker setup *very* well and did my homework years ago.

But it wasn't always this way. The first six months of my career, EVERY CD project was reviewed in a car. As I constantly reviewed these songs on a car stereo, my brain learned how they correlated to my studio speaker setup. I soon learned X amount of bass, brightness, etc. on my setup will sound good in a car and all other mediums.

I still review CDs in a car or do a quick headphone listen from time to time to stay fresh, but I no longer need to do it for every project.

How To Create A Cohesive CD

In other words, how do you create a CD where each song fits together from song to song, all having similar sonic qualities?

I had to come back and address this topic since most people think it's the *only thing* audio mastering is. So, it's important.

The reason I initially forgot to cover this is because if you use the **ReplayGain software** you can easily make all the song volumes on a CD exactly the same.

And once I bring each song as close as possible to industry standard, they all pretty much sonically sound the same. **The CD is automatically cohesive.** So, I don't need to focus on the CD as a whole.

A client could upload three songs and then the rest of the CD a few months later, and they'll still all sound the same. You don't need all songs at the same time to make a CD cohesive, as long as you bring every song as close as possible to industry standard.

BUT, IT WASN'T ALWAYS THIS WAY FOR ME

Ok, I explained how I currently get all songs on a CD to sound similar. But when I first started out, it wasn't that easy. Your journey in audio mastering might be similar.

When I opened my business in 1999, **I mastered each song the best I could, and then made a CD and listened to it on a car stereo, one song after the other.** I took notes for each song, *not* how they compared to each other, but what each song lacked compared to a commercial industry standard song. I then went back and forth making necessary changes until eventually every song was properly adjusted and sounded as close as possible to a commercial song. It was a long process.

After a year in business, my mastering was much better and most of the songs on the CD were very close to industry standard once I was done mastering.

At that time, I still listened to each song, but this time I compared them against each other. There would always be one or two songs that were slightly sonically off compared to the rest of the CD, and I quickly adjusted them. **This will happen for you too if you follow the information in this book and work hard at it!**

Important Note - You can't use a preset for the entire CD, once you've mastered one song.

For example, let's say the first song on a CD gets a *slight* bass boost to get it where it needs to be (industry standard). What if the next song is very low in bass? Well, it's going to need a *big* bass boost. What if the next song has way too much bass? It's going to get a bass *cut* (the opposite).

If you gave every song on the CD a preset *slight* bass boost (like you used on the first song), this action would be wrong for many of the songs on this CD.

You have to work on each song on a song-by-song basis. No presets! I know I've mentioned this a few times in this book, but too many people look for the easy way out in everything they do. I'm trying to emphasize that it won't work in audio mastering.

AUDIO MASTERING STEP-BY-STEP

You FINALLY made it to the "Audio Mastering Step-By-Step" section! I hope you didn't jump to this section first. Ha!

This section covers my audio mastering session, step-by-step. I use the techniques I've outlined in earlier sections of this book, and explain the logic behind my actions.

If you haven't read anything else in this book, this section might not be of great help to you because I only give vague instructions. For example, I might say, "check the UPPER-MIDS, compress them properly, and then make sure brightness and clarity are correct."

Now you might ask, "Where are the UPPER-MIDS? How do you compress them properly? What compression threshold and ratio do you use? How do you know when brightness and clarity are correct? How do you adjust brightness and clarity? How do you know when the BAND is correct?"

These questions, and hundreds more, are answered in previous sections of this book.

Initial Mastering Template Setup

In this section I'm going to start off with the initial mastering template I use. I start many of the processors either OFF or Neutral. But regardless, this is the initial mastering template I start out with.

A lot of people are looking for the "magic mastering presets." Just open the magic preset template and your entire CD is mastered in an hour. Well, magic mastering presets are to audio, what six-minute abs, the thigh master, and the ab roller are to weight loss. It doesn't exist! Especially if you use my template. Most of the processors are off until I evaluate the mix.

Now, I can say roughly 25% of the songs I work on greatly benefit from my preset template "as is." This is why auto mastering programs like LANDR can improve *some* songs. This is also the saying, "even a broken watch is right twice a day."

But, many of the songs I work on need a lot of work. The preset template settings are drastically changed.

My initial mastering template is just that. An initial starting point. You have to start somewhere.

Here are the settings I use when I start an audio mastering project:

All processors have slightly different names for their controllers.

1. 4-BAND FREQUENCY RANGES - Here's where I initially set the frequency bands on all of my Multi-Band Processors.

LOW Band (20hz-130hz), **LOWER-MIDS** (130hz-1,5k), **UPPER-MIDS** (1.5k-9k), **HIGH Band** (9k-20k)

2. Standard 5-Band Equalizer - NO SETTINGS. Even though I use this processor in 90% of the projects I work on. I start with it at neutral until I start mastering.

3. Mid-Side Equalizer - NO SETTINGS. This processor is very rarely used (under 5%). I start with it at OFF unless I end up using.

4. Multi-Band Reverb - NO SETTINGS. This processor is very rarely used (under 5%). I start with it at OFF unless I end up using.

5. Multi-Band Compressor -

For "ALL" BANDS (LIMIT & EXPAND)

THRESHOLD - Limit 0, Expand -50
RATIO - Limit 5, Expand 1.5

"Individual" BANDS (COMPRESSION)

LOW Band - Threshold 50%, Ratio 4 to 1
LOWER-MIDS - Threshold 50%, Ratio 7 to 1
UPPER-MIDS - Threshold 50%, Ratio 4 to 1
HIGH Band - Threshold 50%, Ratio 4 to 1

---

6. Multi-Band Spectral Enhancer (Harmonic Exciter) - ALL BANDS 1 unit, 0 ms delay

7. Multi-Band Stereo Widener - HIGH Band, 10 ms delay, 1 unit

8. Loudness Maximizer - OFF until needed.

On The Song's Effects Bus:

De-esser - NO SETTINGS. I don't even insert this effect unless needed.

Let's Start The Audio Mastering Session

1. It's Time To Get Started!

Along with these step-by-step instructions, use what you've already learned in this book, good A/B comparison, and a solid work ethic to create great audio masters!

2. What File Types Are Used In Audio Mastering?

This has to be mentioned first.

File Types Used In Audio Mastering - .WAV or .AIFF (a single stereo interleaved file).

You *can* master an MP3 but that's like working with 720 STANDARD video instead of 1080 HD video. Why would you?

Sample Rate And Bit Depth - 44.1kHz and (16 or 24 bits) is adequate.

A CD is 44.1kHz and 16 bits. MP3 is the new industry standard and is at a far lower sample rate than 44.1kHz. There's really no reason to master a file any higher than 44.1kHz, since it's eventually going to get converted down for the consumer. Unless of course the client demands it, which happens about 1% of the time for me.

Note - Now, there is mastering for iTunes which requires a huge 96khz file. If you're mastering for this format, obviously you will need to work at a 96khz sample rate.

3. Import Files

A. First off, *open* the INITIAL TEMPLATE we created.

B. *Set* your file TYPE (.Wav, .Aiff, etc.), and *remove* BPM TEMPO CODE (if your DAW software allows it).

C. *Import* **the SONG MIX FILE and** *convert* **it to 44.1khz / 16 bit.**

The reason I always convert all files is because sometimes a client uses a couple different sample rates for their CD, or they send me remixes in a different sample rate. If I convert everything to 44.1khz / 16 bit right off the bat, it makes mastering life a bit easier.

D. I always insert (start) the song file to 0:05 (instead of 0:00). This is so I have room to set the front locator at 0.25-0.5 seconds *before* the start of the song file.

E. *Cut* **the front of the file about 0.25 seconds before the song starts.** There's usually silence there.

Even if you don't see anything, be sure to listen from the very beginning of the file before cutting. Sometimes a song fades in slowly and the audio content is not visible.

Note - 0.5 second TOTAL silent time is the absolute minimum. Sometimes if you go under 0.5 seconds, eventually when you make a CD, the first note of the song will be cut off. You might not even notice it until a client makes a CD on their own, gets it duplicated, and then notifies you about a few songs being cutoff. **Which is a disaster! It's not worth taking the risk.**

F. Import your A/B comparison industry standard reference track.

Make sure it's the same genre with comparable instrumentation. Don't use a reference track with 6 vocal/instrument tracks if the song you're mastering has 30!

4. Visually Evaluate The Song Mix File

A. The next step is to visually evaluate the song mix. This might tell you a few things about how to tackle the project. In this section I will show a few typical file types.

GOOD – This file is good (provided it wasn't recorded disorted). It has +6dbs of headroom in the verses and +3dbs in the choruses. A lot of headroom to do whatever you need to. This is considered by *most* the perfect amount of headroom.

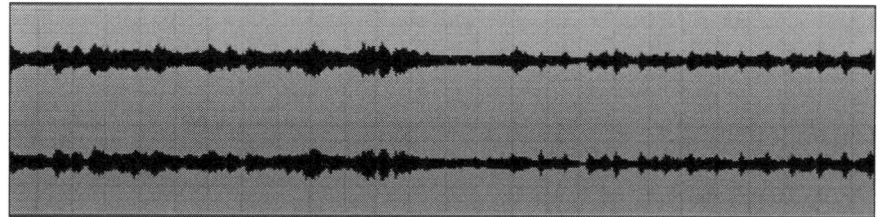

VERY LOW - This song's overall levels are very low (roughly +12dbs of headroom). In this scenario, I just gain the entire song up +12dbs and master it. This will not negatively affect audio quality. It's not worth me sending it back to the client for a louder remix.

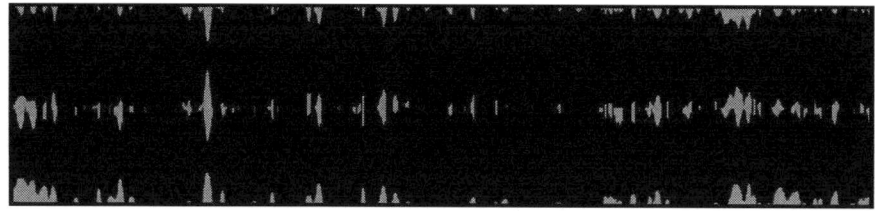

DISTORTED - This file is over-level and more than likely distorted, with no dynamic range. There's an 80% chance you won't be able to master it, and the client will need to reduce their levels and upload a new mix.

Once in a while (20% of the time) I see a hip-hop song that looks just like this and it's *not* distorted. It barely makes it. This is why *listening* is a must before rejecting a song mix.

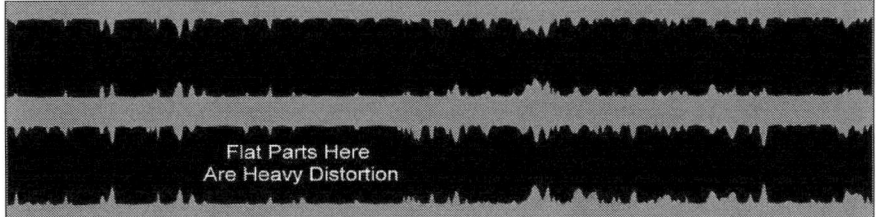

DISTORTED AND GAINED DOWN - This file is the exact same file as the "distorted" one above, but it's gained down -3dbs. I get this once in a while.

During mixing, the song track levels were originally over 0 level and distorted. The client gained the .wav file down (or lowered the master fader) to achieve +6dbs of headroom. It doesn't work that way. All they did was make a distorted song lower in overall volume. It's still distorted and the mastering results will be poor.

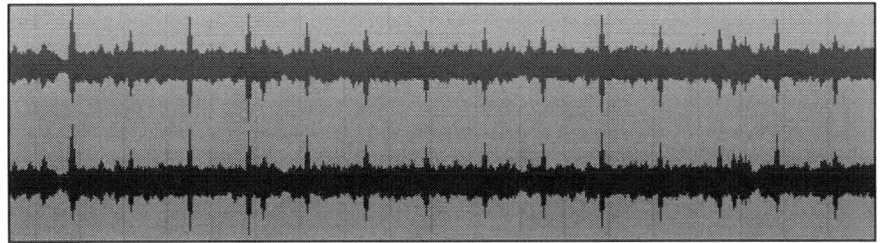

MONO - Yes, there is a left and right channel (which technically means stereo), but notice how the top and bottom waves are 100% *identical*. This means mono. This is one time where *seeing* is better than *hearing*.

Roughly 15% of the mixes I get (especially hip hop) look close to this, because the mixer pans most of the instruments centrally, then uses stereo reverb thinking it will make the song stereo. That doesn't work.

To check for true stereo, use a **Mid-Side EQ** and *solo* the sides. If you did this with the song in the photo above, all you would hear is very light reverb on the outsides of the stereo spectrum.

Unfortunately, a remix request isn't worth it. Most sound engineers that do this to begin with don't have the mixing skills to fix the problem. Especially in hip hop where many times the problem lies in a weak arrangement. You can't get a good stereo mix when all you have is a lead vocal, kick, snare and hi hat. There isn't much to pan to the outsides!

Note - Someone pointed out to me that most of the .wav files on this page look MONO. I agree, they are. The difference is, this one is pretty much 90% MONO. The other .wav files on this page are more like 70%. Still not good....

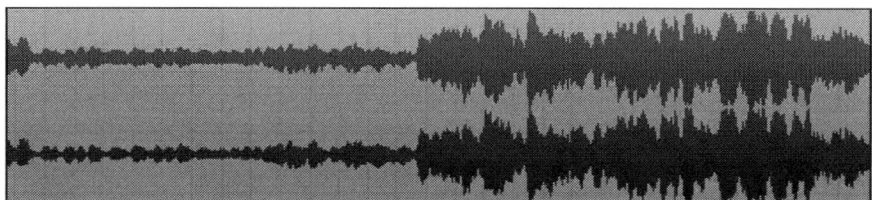

TOO MUCH DYNAMIC RANGE (ERRATIC) BETWEEN SECTIONS - The problem with this song is the chorus is +10db louder than the verses. There's way too much dynamic range here and the volume of your verses will always be too low (even after Loudness Maximization).

The solution is to highlight the verses and gain them all up about +5dbs. It works every time! And no, I wouldn't send it back to the client for a remix when I can fix it myself in a minute.

I cover this in detail in the section, "How To Handle A Song That Has Erratic Sonic Qualities."

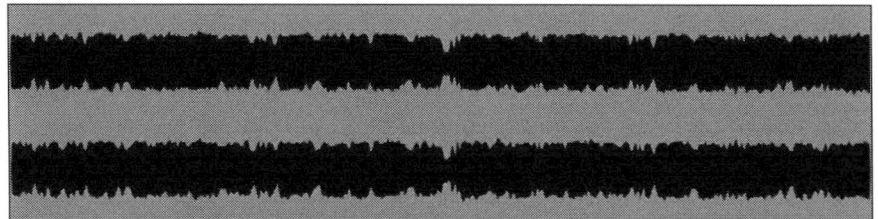

ENTIRE SONG COMPRESSED - This song is compressed from beginning to end. I'm not saying this is necessarily a bad thing. My point is, you won't have to compress this song very much during mastering, if any. A lot of rock songs look like this.

MASTERING FOR CLIENTS TIP - Anything you can fix with editing or in audio mastering, fix it. Don't request a remix unless absolutely necessary. You might lose a client when they can't make the adjustments.

B. NOW I TAKE ACTION - If there's anything mentioned above that needs to be addressed, I address it now. Like gaining the entire song or certain sections, or a must needed remix request, etc.

5. Use Your Ears To Evaluate The Song Mix

Next I use my cursor and quickly jump around the song, listening section by section (opening, verses, pre-chorus, chorus, chorus ending, etc.).

What am I listening for?

A. Is the mix completely distorted, super bright in any sections, or are there any other problems that will give me a *very poor* mastering result? **If the answer is yes, I reject it and tell the client what the problems are. And, how to fix them.**

In previous sections I tell you to do the very best you can with every mix, you might be surprised with what you can achieve. Yes, this is true. But here I'm talking about rejecting GRADE "F" mixes (horrendous) that will yield a poor master. If the mix is a GRADE "D," by all means give it your best shot!

B. I check if the sonic qualities in each section are erratic. If they are, I know getting a great audio master is going to be tough.

I cover this in detail in the section, "How To Handle A Song That Has Erratic Sonic Qualities."

C. I do a very quick overall initial assessment of the main sonic qualities (bass, boominess, thickness, brightness, clarity).

D. I give a quick SOLO listen to each BAND, as part of the evaluation process.

You won't know what corrective actions to take unless you fully evaluate the song you're working on.

6. Slightly Compress Each Of The 4 Bands

Each BAND *already* has a compression THRESHOLD and RATIO setting from the initial mastering template. But since the overall volume of every song will vary, the current THRESHOLD settings are worthless, and need to be adjusted.

A. Using the Multi-Band Compressor, *adjust* the THRESHOLDS to 60% on ALL 4 BANDS. Note – During the LOUDEST part of the song.

IMPORTANT - Keep ALL The Other Initial Compressor Settings (Ratio, Attack, Release, etc) AS IS.

I want each BAND to have a slight amount of compression to start with.

If you don't understand my THRESHOLD percentages, please read the section "Working With A Compressor's Threshold And Ratio Settings."

7. Loudness Maximize The Song

The next step is to **Loudness Maximize** the song.

A. *Set* the THRESHOLD a little below the very peak of the song meter. If you're using the Ozone **loudness maximizer**, take the THRESHOLD down to where the meter starts getting thick. You're trying to get the song within 1-2dbs of the final volume.

This is VERY important to do early in the mastering process, because when a song is made *louder*, it changes sonically. It definitely gets harsher overall and hotter in the UPPER-MIDS.

If you spend a lot of time mastering a song at a very low volume output level, and then make a big boost (+8dbs or more) with the **loudness maximizer**, the song's sonic qualities will change so dramatically you're basically starting from scratch in the mastering process.

Get your output volume levels close to the final output level ASAP so you know what you're working with!

Note- I'm referring to the **output level of the song**, *NOT* the **volume level coming out of your speakers**. The speaker volume level does make a difference, but I am not referring to that here.

8. Adjust Anything Moderately Sonically Off

A. I quickly listen to the song mix and adjust any sonic qualities that are moderately off. I already have in my mind what I would like to do from my initial visual and audio evaluations.

I'm not doing an exact A/B comparison to a reference track at this time. I'm just trying to get the audio master closer to industry standard by quickly fixing *obvious* sonic problems.

For example, I immediately recognize the bass is way too loud (+5dbs) so I *cut* it. The cymbals and hi hats are a big scratchy hiss, so I *lower* their volume, etc.

I guess you could call this prep work. Kind of like an auto body repair guy. Right now we're banging out the major dents and maybe adding some Bondo. Later, we'll sand everything down, spray paint and clear coat (the final master).

9. Initial Master (Speaker Monitor Volume)

I always do two masters.

A. On the first pass, I master at a lower speaker volume level of around 85dbs.
B. The second master and tweak ends with loud playback (100-105dbs) over a very short period of time (maybe a minute a song max).

Another Mastering Law -

You CANNOT correctly master a song for loud playback unless you master it while it's being played loud.

Another no-brainer, but 80% of the songs I get back from other studios for remasters are horrendous when played back loud. They obviously never turned up the volume and checked their work. Probably because so many sound engineers have their monitor speakers on the desk a foot from their faces. They can't turn the music up loud!

Yes, I always do two masters on each song with an extended break in-between. For example, after initially mastering a 12 song CD, I will not listen to any music for at least 4-6 hours. After this period, I revisit the songs and do a final second master and tweak. Or, I'll do the second master and tweak the next day on completely fresh ears.

Using this *fresh ear* approach, when I revisit the songs its like a lightbulb goes off in my head! Any tiny sonic details that I'm slightly off on become 100% apparent and I quickly adjust them.

Initially Setting Up Your Bands

In the upcoming pages, I'm going to discuss initially setting up your BANDS.

This process is kind of like putting on a car tire. You first "loosely" screw on all the bolts, getting them *close* to where they need to be. You then straighten out the tire and tighten the bolts a bit more (one by one), before locking them all down real tight. You don't put the tire on and then lock down ONE bolt! If you did, the tire could be crooked and all the other bolts would be off.

The same goes for mastering. You try to get the sonic qualities in each BAND "close" to where they need to be. Then listen to what you have as a whole before tweaking and adjusting everything (maybe a few times). Finally at the end, you tighten everything up, just like the tire.

10. Setting The UPPER-MIDS (1k - 9k)

When it comes to the equalization of a song, there are two main components that everyone knows. Bass and treble. **The UPPER-MIDS is where a song's treble resides.**

If you are familiar with *mixing* (I think most of you are) you know you have to have a starting point, and then you build around it.

In mixing, I start with the kick and bass relationship, and then add the snare and my metal percussion rhythms. Once this is all set in relation to each other, I then begin adding other elements that work around this starting point.

Many sound engineers mix this exact same way. If they don't, they still have to start with some sonic element of choice and build around it. And whatever they choose, they usually start the same way every time.

Well, in audio mastering I start with the UPPER-MIDS. At least half of the vocal frequencies reside here, along with most of the lead guitar and main music melodies. These are all main focal points of the listener. **This is also where a song's brightness and clarity comes from.**

A. Working in the UPPER-MIDS, now's the time to A/B compare between the song you're mastering and your industry standard reference track.

Determine what sounds different. Go through all your UPPER-MID sonic qualities (brightness, clarity, separation, vocal presence). What does your master lack compared to the reference track? Or does it have too much of something?

B. Use all the information I gave you in previous sections to bring the UPPER-MIDS as close as possible to your reference track. Just keep going back and forth (A/B comparing) and apply the proper effects. Little by little you'll get closer to the reference track.

This initial UPPER-MIDS setting isn't the "end all be all". It will be adjusted again. **You just want a solid starting point to work around with the other BANDS.**

Important Note - I'm not going to keep mentioning this in every section, but it does need to be mentioned one more time. **When A/B comparing, or when generally reviewing your song master, be sure to SOLO your BANDS.**

If something sounds strange or is sonically incorrect in my master, I SOLO the offending BAND to get a closer listen. For example, if the song isn't bright enough, I SOLO the UPPER-MIDS to get a closer listen. If the kick and bass sound muffled, I SOLO the LOW Band to hear if they're colliding. **Getting each BAND right means the entire song as a whole will be right!**

11. Setting The LOW Band (20hz - 150hz)

When it comes to the equalization of a song, there are two main components that everyone knows. Bass and treble. **The LOW Band is your bass.**

A. Next, I set the bass *volume* and *boominess* (using the techniques I've outlined in this book). Back to A/B comparison to get them where they need to be for the song's genre.

I don't really focus on the song as a whole yet. At this time I *do not* go back and forth between the LOW Band and UPPER-MIDS and balancing them against each other. That comes later in the process.

My first two steps are to get the UPPER-MIDS and LOW Band relatively close to the reference track. We've just completed both.

12. Setting The LOWER-MIDS (150hz - 1.5k)

Ok, the treble (UPPER-MIDS) and bass (LOW Band) are initially set. **The LOWER-MIDS are a bridge between the LOW Band and UPPER-MIDS.**

A. I adjust the LOWER-MIDS so they complement both BANDS.

Note - I don't rely on a reference track here. It's all about making this BAND work with the LOW Band and UPPER-MIDS.

The LOWER-MIDS can provide thickness, warmth and presence to the song.

This is also the BAND where mud could reside. If the LOWER-MIDS are too loud, thick, or distorted they could run over the UPPER-MIDS and greatly reduce the master's clarity and brightness. Watch out for this.

A good portion of the bass line (or synth bass line) resides here. If a song has a prominent bass/synth line and it's weak in the song mix, it might need to be *boosted* using the **5-Band Standard EQ**.

If the LOWER-MIDS are very harsh or washed out mud, they might need to be thinned out or the volume might need to be reduced.

Working with over 30,000 songs, I've found that roughly 65% of the time the LOWER-MIDS sound great using only a slight amount of compression, and leaving everything else "as is." This is common.

13. Setting The HIGH Band (9k - 20k)

The other three BANDS are set.

A. Now we *set* the HIGH Band.

My main focus in this BAND is volume control. I make sure the hi hat & cymbal combination isn't too bright/thick or isn't too low in volume. I don't want the hi hat rhythm to disappear.

If this BAND is problematic, you might have to slide the BAND range to the left a bit (to around 7k) before correcting it.

As I've mentioned a few times, I always *add* some **stereo widening** to the HIGH Band. This BAND usually doesn't contain much audio content, but it could add that needed extra sparkle.

14. Check Volume And Adjust

We've done several mastering steps, and the overall volume level of the song has changed. I need to get it close to the final output level again, since any volume change will alter the song's sonic qualities.

A. Next step, I *export* the song. Then, *import* the file into **ReplayGain** and *check* the volume level.

B. After checking the volume level I adjust it using the Loudness Maximizer. Everything is fairly relative. Not exact, but close. If **ReplayGain** says 96 and I need the song to be 98, I add +2 on the THRESHOLD of the **Loudness Maximizer**. That should get you close to 98 (give or take a 1/2 db).

15. Listen To The Song As A Whole And Adjust

Its time to start tightening up the bolts!

A. Now's the time I listen to the song as a whole and do a good *overall* A/B comparison to my reference track, making adjustments as needed.

I preview at around 85-90dbs but will jump up to 105dbs periodically for 3-5 seconds to loosely adjust for loud playback. In this step, I work more in the 85-90db range. In step #17, I focus more on loud playback.

Note - As mentioned in the previous section "How To Handle Songs With Erratic Sonic Qualities," be sure to compensate if needed.

Here are a few things I'm listening for:

First I focus on the UPPER-MIDS. I need correct brightness, with a nice tone. I want clarity and compression to sound good. Can I hear the vocals well? Do the lead guitars have a nice tone?

Is my bass loudness and boominess right? If there's a bass line melody, is it loud enough?

Is my hi hat/cymbal volume correct? Is the hi hat rhythm loud enough to carry the song tempo?

Is the song thick enough or is it too thick? Is the song tinny or brittle bright?

Distortion should already be removed in a previous step, if not, do I hear any?

Do any overly bright sections or instruments jump out of the song?

Is the MID instrumentation loud enough compared to the song as a whole, or should it be boosted?

Are any of the BANDS interfering with another BAND, running it over? Do they compliment each other?

Is the song wide enough? Does the song have a nice sparkle to it?

Is there a sharp Sss sound in the vocals or a pinchy bright sound in the music that I should De-ess or EQ cut?

B. Next I sit back and listen to the song as I would a song that's on the radio. I listen as a *music lover*, not as a sound engineer. Does the song sound "*GOOD?*" **If not, WHY DOESN'T IT?**

C. After closely listening, I make minor tweaks as needed, bringing the audio master as close as possible to greatness!

16. Break Time!

Ok, the initial master is done! Time for a break.

I might work on another initial master or an entire CD, but **I will not revisit *this song* for at least 4-6 hours, if not the next day.**

17. 2nd Master And Tweak On Fresh Ears

Its time to lock down the bolts!

Here's where I start the final master and tweak. The break and fresh ears allows me to quickly notice any mistakes I've made on the first mastering pass.

Usually at this point in the audio mastering process, major changes are not needed. Just a few minor tweaks to take an audio master from very good to great!

But, if you're new at this, you might have to give your masters a *few* fresh listens (coming back to it several times) and make bigger changes. That's ok, just get it right.

Also, if I do have a problem, it's usually in the UPPER-MIDS. On fresh ears I can quickly tell if they're too bright or not bright enough, and then I dial in a nice tone.

A. While doing the second master and tweak, I start out at around 90dbs and repeat the mastering process (going through my sonic qualities checklist again). Most of them will already be right on.

B. Once the master sounds good at this volume, I then move up to 100-105dbs (for 3-5 seconds at a time) to make sure **the loudest part of the song** doesn't *break up* at a loud volume and still sounds good overall.

At this time I pretty much ALWAYS need to adjust the compressor THRESHOLD on the UPPER-MIDS. If even a slight amount.

Important Note - Once you get your master right for loud playback, *it's automatically* good for low volume play back. You don't have to go back down to a low volume and adjust again.

C. I then give the song a listen on headphones to see how it translates there. I very slightly adjust as needed. Nothing major. I don't want to mess up my speaker master.

D. If you're going to listen in a car, now's the time. The car stereo is the ultimate listening environment to judge stereo spread (which is primarily a mixing issue).

Mixing note - If you're doing your own mixing and your song is weak in the stereo field, remember this rule. **You can't have any sound coming from the outside of the stereo field *unless you have something panned there!*** If you have only light stereo reverb there, that doesn't count.

18. The Final Export - Loudness Maximization

This is the final step in the mastering process.

A. I *check* the song's volume a final time with **ReplayGain** and use the **Loudness Maximizer** to set the volume where it should be.

Important Note That Needs To Be Repeated -

If you're working with a song that has erratic volume levels from section to section (+6dbs or more of dynamic range), **set your locators *ONLY* before and after the loudest section and export *ONLY* that small section.** Your volume level assessments should be based *only* on the loudest section of the song. If not, you could get a false reading from **ReplayGain,** and I can just about guarantee you will distort on the loud sections.

And of course, *never* export only the lower volume sections of a song (which defies common sense). That will obviously give you a false reading and distortion.

On the flip side, if the song has +5dbs or less of dynamic range, set your locators to include at least one verse and the loudest part of the song and you will get a spot on average volume reading.

B. *Cut* **the end of the song and** *fade out* **as needed.** Be sure to listen very closely for a click at the very end. If you get one, just cut it off.

You're done. If it's for a client, wait for their great response!

C. IMPORTANT - After making ANY adjustments to this master, a client mix swap, etc., be sure to check and adjust your overall volume levels. Just cutting your treble a bit could change the song's average volume and put you -1db under industry standard. **You cannot have this happen!**

MASTERING FOR CLIENTS TIP - If you're working with clients and giving out free demos or have a money-back guarantee, export only 2-3 minutes of the song as a partial preview. If you give them the entire song, everyone will lie and say they don't like it and you'll never get paid! Ha!

During the busy season, I'll get at least one person a week who will say after getting the free partial demo, "Something's wrong, you didn't upload the full song." Oh, really? You never paid anything! How long would I be in business if I gave everyone full free songs? They'll laugh and say, "Right, my bad."

MASTERING DIFFERENT GENRES

In this chapter I will discuss the specific sonic qualities of over a dozen different genres.

How Do *I* Know The Sonic Qualities For Each Genre?

This might be a dumb question, but I wanted you to know it's not *only* from years of experience and A/B comparison using industry standard songs. Customer feedback from over 7,500 clients has also played a big part in writing these sonic quality pages, and this entire book.

Why would you even care? Because if you are working with clients, my sonic quality overviews and advice are going to satisfy most of them since it's largely based on their feedback.

Also, since I've worked with so many real clients and songs, you're getting solid real-world information. Not theory.

Surfing the net, you will find many sound engineering and online teachers have *very little* real-world positive experience. Some haven't even worked with very many customers! All they have is book theory or what they learned in school, or from a course.

Granted some of them have made TONS of money selling courses, but that's because they aren't good enough to actually mix or master someone else's music, so they can't get any business! They can't properly mix or master a song for someone else, but they can take your money and tell you how to do it. Ha!

Its kind of like the "make a million a year with no money down" flipping houses infomercial guys. They personally make millions telling you *how* to do this, but they've never made a dime doing it themselves. And you won't either...

LEARNING SONIC QUALITIES YOURSELF

I had to come back and add more to this section because I felt I minimized the value of song study. Along with reading this book, you need to study the sonic characteristics of the genres you will be working on.

I began my in-depth song study back in the mid 90's. I was arranging and creating music at the time. Learning the instrumentation used in my genre was a must. I also needed to learn general rhythm patterns for each instrument and what function each one played in the arrangement.

Mixing had its own set of learning challenges. I had to learn instrument and vocal volume levels (in relation to each other), stereo field panning, what effects were being used on each audio element, and overall balance. This all needed to be studied and was learned by breaking down commercial songs on the radio, reading books, videos, etc.

And last, there was audio mastering. Which is mostly about fine tuning a song's overall sonic qualities. Hey, that's a new definition for audio mastering!

If you want to be great at audio mastering, you can't just A/B compare everything you work on your entire life. You need to closely listen to commercial songs in every genre, listening from a "sonic qualities" viewpoint. Learn each genres brightness level, bass volume, boominess, compression/dynamic level, etc.

IMPORTANT - Be sure to SOLO EACH BAND as part of your study. How should the UPPER-MIDS sound in a good commercial song? How should the LOWER-MIDS sound in a good commercial song?

One thing you'll notice during this exercise is how the LOW Band in commercial songs sound clear. You can hear the bass/synth and kick as two separate instruments.

When I SOLO the LOW Band of a client's song, most of the time its undefined and muffled, why is this? Because most clients poorly high and low pass filter their mixes, which means there's a lot of instrumentation bleed. The bass guitar bleeds into the kick and low part of the vocals, creating a LOW Band muffle.

Vocals And Instrumentation May Change Your Sonic Approach

Each main genre of music has its own specific sonic qualities. But you also have sub-genres whose sonic qualities slightly vary from the main genre.

What I'm trying to say here is the sonic qualities I give you for each main genre could vary.

THE SINGER'S SONG

The singer's song presents another problem. This has happened to me so many times I should have made it an audio mastering law! **If you're mastering a singer's song, you have to treat it differently from a compression and dynamic standpoint.**

By *singer's song* I mean a song where the vocals are the main focus, and the music is secondary. For example, a choir singing gospel, an R&B song or love ballad with a great powerful singer, a pop song with a powerful vocal track, or a singer-songwriter song that has only vocals and guitar. Even though there are no vocals, you can throw classical music and orchestral movie soundtracks into this conversation too.

When working with these types of songs, what I've experienced is the client *always* wants very little or no compression in the UPPER-MIDS, and a lower overall volume (97-97.5).

They want a natural bright uncompressed sound in the vocal area (UPPER-MIDS). They want everyone to be able to "hear" their great vocal abilities.

Is it right to do this? Not exactly. If you listen to similar pro-mastered commercial songs and play them loud, the peaks are cut off with compression, so they don't break up or burn your ears. **But, you'll find *clients* don't want this.**

When I'm faced with this situation, the client gets two initial mastering previews. One, that's properly mastered the way it should be. The second, the way they want it, with very little compression in the UPPER-MIDS and with the overall volume a little lower.

I briefly explain why they're getting two masters, then run with the version they choose. Most of the time they go with the very little compression version, or request that I remove all compression.

Note - This situation usually works with the client, unlike the "match the client reference track" scenario that hardly ever works.

Why not just give them the song the way it's supposed to be mastered? You're the expert. Aren't you supposed to make every song sound the very best it can? Good questions. The answer is because at least 70% of the clients will reject it. And because a light compression and lower volume preference isn't a terrible preference request.

If you're running a studio that gives out free demos, the client isn't going to email you back and tell you to reduce compression and overall volume. They're just going to use another sound engineer who didn't compress it (usually because they don't know how to do it in the first place).

Of course if you're mastering your own music, you go with the *correct* sonic qualities I outline in this book.

How To Master Different Genres

Here's my mastering approach based on over 30,000 songs I've mastered since 1999. Instead of just giving you a basic synopsis of the song genre, I felt detailing the main sonic qualities would keep everything more organized.

This section not only gives you my mastering approach for the genre, I also factor in client feedback so your masters will make them happy too. **But remember, A/B comparison and matching is always your goal.** This section assists you in doing that.

CLARITY & SEPARATION (FOR ALL GENRES)

Regardless of the genre, each instrument and vocal should have its own space, allowing you to clearly hear everything. You should be able to understand at least 90% of the vocals (if not 100%). Unfortunately, if a mix is very crowded, little can be done in mastering to correct it (though I do encourage *trying* to fix the problem).

How To Master Metal And Hard Rock

Ratings - I rate each sonic quality on a scale from 1-10 (5 is an average amount). Except for overall loudness, I use my ReplayGain recommended levels.

Clarity (5) The guitars are usually bright and thick, so you're not going to get the same clarity you would from a song with thinner instrumentation.

The vocals should cut through nicely, but most clients in this genre purposely want the vocals under the music a bit because they're usually not very good singers. This is ok *if* you can understand most of the vocals. If you can't understand 20% or more, the client should fix it. If they refuse, be sure to emphasize you made them aware of a serious vocal problem and they refused to correct it.

You don't want them coming back later and either bad mouthing your mastering, or asking for a refund.

Brightness (8)
Metal and hard rock are the brightest of the major genres because of the thick stereo guitars. They're the *brightest*, but make sure you A/B compare well, not to go *too bright*. This music is played loud!

The *tone* of the guitar brightness is very important. You want a nice full bright sound with some bite to it, not thin and tinny bright.

Bass Volume & Boominess (4 or 6 the new hard rock)
I don't want the bass too boomy. I do often add some boominess to this genre, but only to thicken up the song if its too thin. I want the bass to be felt and have presence, but just loud enough so you can barely hear it. I *never* want a ringing boomy bass (like in hip hop). This applies to *most* hard rock songs.

The exception to this rule is hard rock with the big powerful double kick (the new hard rock). You want to be able to hear and feel this. These songs aren't just about the guitars. The big bass is important too.

Overall Compression (7)
These genres are played loud, so I can't have them breaking up. Using the **Multi-Band Compressor** in the UPPER-MIDS, I always cut the top off.

Even though this is a loud genre that needs compression, if you're working with clients, *most* of the time rock is compressed very well by whoever mixed it. You can usually tell just by looking at the .wav file. Slight or no compression is required if this is the case.

Stereo Width (7)
A nice stereo width is very important for the stereo guitars.

Overall Loudness ReplayGain Number (99-99.5)
Metal/hard rock and hip/hop rap are the loudest genres. This recommended volume works well.

How To Master Classic Rock

Ratings - I rate each sonic quality on a scale from 1-10 (5 is an average amount). Except for overall loudness, I use my ReplayGain recommended levels.

Clarity (5)
Classic rock has an average amount of clarity. It's not a bright genre and warmth is important. I want clarity in all genres, but other genres will have a lot more.

Brightness (5)
Classic rock has an average amount of brightness. You definitely don't want your master to be too bright and digital sounding, losing its warmth.

Bass Volume & Boominess (6)
Of all the rock genres, classic rock has the most bass. I'll go a little over an average amount of bass volume and boominess, which adds warmth to the song. Especially if the song has a prominent bass line.

Overall Compression (4)
I keep compression a little lighter than usual. Classic rock isn't played as loud as other genres, it's not very bright, and dynamic range is appreciated.

Classic rock is the *opposite* of loud and smashed. Lower volume and nice dynamics is the goal.

Stereo Width (6)
Classic rock is a little wider than average. You want a nice stereo guitar sound.

Overall Loudness ReplayGain Number (97-97.5)
Classic rock is -1.5db to -2dbs lower than hard rock. Clients who make classic rock are *not* into the loudness wars. They want their music to sound like classic rock sounded in the 70's, before loudness maximizers were created!

How To Master Pop-Rock, Punk, Alternative, And Country

Ratings - I rate each sonic quality on a scale from 1-10 (5 is an average amount). Except for overall loudness, I use my ReplayGain recommended levels.

Clarity (6)
These genres have slightly above average clarity. The vocals play a major role and need to be understood, unlike hard rock where many times the vocalist doesn't mind their vocals being crowded in and hidden a bit.

Brightness (6)
Brightness is slightly above average. These genres could be played back loud and you don't want them too bright.

Bass Volume & Boominess (6)
I put this sonic quality rating at slightly above average because it pretty much depends on the song.

If the song is a standard rock, your bass could be only a 5. But if the song has a dominant bass-line, you might be looking at a 6-7.

Overall Compression (6)
Once again, right above the middle. A little less compression than hard rock, but more than classic rock (which is very low).

Stereo Width (7)
Many times these genres will have stereo guitars. So, a nice stereo width is very important.

Overall Loudness ReplayGain Number (98-98.5)
The volume level of these genres are a step below hard rock and hip-hop. This helps them maintain a little more dynamic range, which is important because they're usually more musical than the aforementioned genres.

How To Master Hip-Hop And Rap

Ratings - I rate each sonic quality on a scale from 1-10 (5 is an average amount). Except for overall loudness, I use my ReplayGain recommended levels.

Clarity (7)
Hip-hop and rap songs are very clear. They're basically bright & clear with a big boomy bass. The lack of prominent LOWER-MIDS is the reason why.

Brightness (7)
Hip-hop and rap are pretty bright genres. They need to be because the bass is so big, the vocals and UPPER-MID instruments need to be bright enough to cut through.

Bass Volume & Boominess (9)
The boomiest and biggest bass of all genres! You want that sub-bass to ring loud.

The LOWER-MIDS don't play much of a part in hip-hop and rap. I don't want the song to be thin and tinny, but usually the big boomy bass in the LOW Band is enough to give the song its thickness.

Overall Compression (8)
These genres are played loud, so I can't have then breaking up.

Stereo Width (5)
You never want a narrow song, but many times hip-hop and rap mixes don't have much audio material on the outsides (which means a mono sounding mix).

If you're working with clients, you'll get in a lot of hip hop mixes that are stereo files, but sound mono.

Overall Loudness ReplayGain Number (99-99.5)
Metal/hard rock and hip/hop rap are the loudest genres. This recommended volume works well.

How To Master R&B

Ratings - I rate each sonic quality on a scale from 1-10 (5 is an average amount). Except for overall loudness, I use my ReplayGain recommended levels.

Clarity (6)
The vocals are very important in R&B, so you definitely want the song to be clean and clear.

Brightness (6)
A little above average brightness is good. You want to retain some warmth and you definitely don't want the song to be tinny or thin.

Bass Volume & Boominess (7)
R&B songs usually have a nice bass line and a nice kick that thumps. You want to make sure you can hear and feel them, but not to the extent that they muddy up the vocal track.

Overall Compression (4)
Here's where a bit of controversy comes in. Myself personally, I cut the top off with a high THRESHOLD in the UPPER-MIDS. This is what's done with commercial songs, and this is the correct way to do it. But you'll find a lot of clients from this genre want no compression.

My previous article "Vocals And Instrumentation May Change Your Sonic Approach" talks more about this situation.

Stereo Width (6)
Some R&B songs have jazz type music backing (more width), some are more hip-hop with synth pads (not as wide).

Overall Loudness ReplayGain Number (98-98.5)
R&B volumes are comparable to pop, dance, pop-rock, EDM, etc. (not real loud, but not low either). You want to retain some dynamic range.

How To Master Pop-Dance, EDM, And Synth

Ratings - I rate each sonic quality on a scale from 1-10 (5 is an average amount). Except for overall loudness, I use my ReplayGain recommended levels.

Clarity (6)
These genres have slightly above average clarity. When arranged and mixed properly, the bright synth melodies are crisp and clear. When they're not, it's a bright stereo reverbed mash of noise.

Brightness (6)
Brightness is slightly above average. I say this because most of the instrumentation is naturally bright. Songs from these genres are played loud in clubs, so you don't want them too bright.

Bass Volume & Boominess (6)
Pop-dance is a little more boomy (6-7), while EDM and synth heavy music uses a dryer bass that has more punch and less boominess (5-6).

Overall Compression (7)
These genres are played loud, so I can't have them breaking up.

Using the **Multi-Band Compressor** in the UPPER-MIDS, I always cut the top off. I start out with the THRESHOLD at around 40% (and a RATIO of 8:1 to start with) and then work the THRESHOLD up until the song starts breaking up at loud volume playback. Tweak your RATIO as needed.

Stereo Width (7)
These genres usually have layered stereo synth melodies somewhere in the song that would sound very weak if they were narrow. You want a nice stereo spread.

Overall Loudness ReplayGain Number (98-98.5)
These genres are a step below hard rock and hip-hop volume levels. This helps them maintain a little more dynamic range which is important because they're usually more musical than the aforementioned genres.

How To Master Movie Soundtrack, Classical, And Jazz

Ratings - I rate each sonic quality on a scale from 1-10 (5 is an average amount). Except for overall loudness, I use my ReplayGain recommended levels.

Clarity (6)
Each genre could vary, but overall they all have that "big warm sound" in common.

Brightness (6)
This genre has a slightly above average amount of brightness, mainly because the instrumentation could include violins, bright trumpets, chimes, etc. You definitely don't want your master to be too bright and digital sounding, losing its warmth.

Most clients from this genre aren't very good at high and low pass filtering their instruments. They basically mix all their instruments raw "as is" which leaves the entire mix thick, and the UPPER-MID instruments peaking too brightly.

I've found *cutting* **EQ** around 2-3k will usually soften and cure this bright peaking problem.

Bass Volume & Boominess (6)
I put this sonic quality at slightly above average because it pretty much depends on the song.

If there are big booming kettle drums throughout most of the song, or maybe there's a big bass jazz solo, you might be looking at 7-8 for bass and boominess.

All the genre's in this section need warmth, and extra bass helps with that. So, you definitely don't want the bass to be below average.

Overall Compression (4)
Here's where a bit of controversy comes in. Myself personally, I cut the top off with a high THRESHOLD in the UPPER-MIDS. This is what's done with commercial songs and this is the correct way to do it. But you'll find a lot of clients want no compression in these genres.

My previous article "Vocals And Instrumentation May Change Your Sonic Approach" talks more about this situation.

Stereo Width (8)   These genres typically have the most instrumentation that fills the entire stereo field. They need to be wide, especially the epic movie soundtracks. I've personally never heard a *narrow* movie sound track, jazz or classical music song.

Overall Loudness ReplayGain Number (97)   This genre is one of the lowest in terms of volume. Sparing usage of the loudness maximizer will make the master warmer and more dynamic.

WORKING WITH CLIENTS

In this chapter, I'm going to give a few *must know* tips pertaining to working with clients.

Should I Ask Clients For A Reference Song?

I saw this question asked on music forums several times. And the answer is always, "Yes, of course. Then you know what the client is looking for." **This is a common sense answer anyone can give,** *not based on actual real world experience.* And it's a very wrong answer...

I've worked with over 7,500 clients since 1999. But, roughly only 200 clients either uploaded a reference track, or told me a band they're trying to sound like. Most of my clients just let me do my thing, without any recommendations.

I'm very good at matching reference songs. Well, a funny thing happened with these 200 clients. **An *astounding* 75% (150 of them) all told me word for word, "Wow, you did a great job matching my reference song, but I don't like it for my song!"** Ha! Then why did you send it to me and tell me to match it?

I really don't know why this happens, and there's no reason to elaborate. I've worked with enough people to know it's a fact. **75% of the time matching a client's reference track doesn't work.**

Armed with this information, if a client gives me a reference track or a band recommendation, I now give them back two masters. One is a reference match, and the other is how *I feel* it should be mastered.

What's the end result? 75% of the time they choose my master.

Just like in any other business, this is just another example of how *real world experience* **trumps common sense and theory.**

Using The Initial Preview As A Reference

Before I start mastering a CD project, the client gets an initial master preview of *one* song. They then give me any preference adjustments. Now I have a master they like, and I *could* make all the songs on the CD similar.

The question is, *should I*? The answer is, *yes* but loosely.

Most clients do well with the initial preview. If they approve it, they usually really do like it. It's rare for them to approve an initial preview, then complain about the entire project that you mastered similarly. This usually only happens if the mixes are very poor, which means the masters are too. If this is the case, you shouldn't have mastered the poor mixes to begin with.

Yes, I import the client's approved initial preview into the project so I can reference it for each song, but when the actual mastering process goes on, I **DO NOT** A/B compare it and try and replicate it *exactly* for every song on the CD. **I still try to replicate an industry standard song for every song in the project.**

I quickly reference the initial preview *only* to make sure all songs are fairly consistent. So all the songs on the CD form a "cohesive unit."

Sometimes the client's initial master does give you an overall preference you can use. For example, if a client says they want a warm, analog sound, and a little lower in volume, they will *immediately* reject a digital sounding loud master. So, these preferences must be used on every song. But then again, this isn't exact matching the initial preview. It's applying a few personal preferences you were given across the board.

Here's why I don't exact replicate the client's approved initial master preview:

1. Sometimes my initial master didn't use the best song mix on the CD. Even though the client approved the initial master and it sounds good, sometimes several other mixes on the CD are better, and will yield better mastering results. **My goal is to make each song sound the very best it can.** I'm not doing that if I'm matching the entire CD to a master I created that used an inferior mix.

2. They might not have evaluated the initial master very well, and gave you bad preference adjustments.

This is rare (maybe 5% of the time), but it does happen. The client gives preference adjustments they don't entirely agree with. If I made every song sound exactly like the initial master preview, they would reject everything.

3. All songs on a CD are slightly different.   They have their own feeling and character. Sometimes the client throws in a few totally different songs. Many times you couldn't match the initial preview to every song even if you wanted too.

Go With The Client's Mix Or With What You Know?

Ok, I have to explain what I'm talking about here. **Many times a client submits a song and the mix is exaggerated in some area.** For example, a hip hop mix has *very heavy* bass, or a rock mix has *super bright* guitars.

So, do you incorporate these exaggerations into your master, or should you master the songs how you know they should sound for their genre?

Well, I used to think that since the bass was very loud or the guitars were very bright in the mix, that's what the client likes, so I'll leave it like that. **WRONG!** When I did that they would come back with, "What's wrong with you dude? These guitars are so bright they're burning my ears! Or, man that's way too much bass."

It's funny because if they "knew" there was way too much bass, why did they mix it that way and send it to me?

Master every song to industry standard. Now, you can lean *slightly* in the direction of the mix, but just a little. Client's don't want a master that's way sonically off, even though their mixes might be.

How To Handle A Very Poor Mix

Just so you know, if you're giving out free demos on your website and a very poor mix is submitted, you have about a 5% chance this demo will convert into a paying customer. Maybe even more like 2%. And if you send them a corrective action for the mix, maybe only 10% will respond. **When it comes to free mastering demos, I reject very poor mixes.** They're a waste of time for everyone.

As for paying clients who submit poor mixes, I email them back what the problem is and have them correct it. It's 50/50 if they can fix it or not. If they can't, they already paid so they'll get a free preview and we'll take it from there.

Here's why I mentioned earlier in the book that you need to learn how to work in decibels. If you can't explain what corrective actions need to be taken on these poor mixes, you might lose a client.

If a client approves a master that I know is not great and they want me to proceed with the entire CD project, I email them a disclaimer stating that all the masters will be similar and will not sound great. This is the time you should tell the client that 50% of the project price is a non-refundable labor fee, or you'll be working for nothing more times than not.

MY MAIN RESOURCES

Visit my online studio **JRmastering.com** and save 25%

HomeStudioGearSecrets.com – Checkout my best home studio gear picks for 2020!

BestMusicHosting.com – My pick for the best music website hosting. I've used this company for over 10 years for all of my websites. Only $4.95 a month.

Check out my latest books - Available on Amazon.

New customers visit my online studio **JRmastering.com** and save 25%

AMS VIDEO Course

Audio Mastering Secrets Video Course

Lifetime Membership To 5 Hours Of Video

Visit my website AudioMasteringSecrets.com

Thanks and enjoy!

If you have any questions, email me - info@audiomasteringsecrets.com

Thank You!

I would like to thank you for purchasing this book. I hope it has immensely improved your audio mastering skills.

Stay confident, work hard, and keep on learning. After 30 years in music, I still learn a little something here and there every week. **"Learning Is For a Lifetime!"**

I wish you the very best of luck in all that you do! Cheers! God Bless!

Your Friend,

John Rogers

Contact Info

Contact Me - info@JRmastering.com

Follow Me On Twitter - @JRmastering

Copyright 2017

All rights reserved. No part of this publication may be reproduced, distributed, or transmitted in any form or by any means, including photocopying, recording, or other electronic or mechanical methods, without the prior written permission from JR Mastering, except in the case of brief quotations embodied in critical reviews and certain other noncommercial uses permitted by copyright law. For permission requests please email John Rogers at info@JRmastering.com.

Ordering Information:

Special discounts are available on quantity purchases by corporations, associations, and others. For details, contact John Rogers at info@JRmastering.com.

Made in the USA
Monee, IL
20 August 2020